Collins

GUILDFORD

TOWN ATLAS

Contents

Road Map	2-3
Key to Street Map Symbols	4
Key to Street Map Pages	5
Town Centre Map	6-7
Street Maps	8-29
Local Information	30-31
Index to Street Names	32-40

Published by Collins
An imprint of HarperCollinsPublishers
77-85 Fulham Palace Road, Hammersmith, London W6 8JB

Copyright © HarperCollinsPublishers Ltd 2001
Mapping © Bartholomew Ltd 2001

Collins® is a registered trademark of HarperCollinsPublishers Limited

The HarperCollins website address: www.fireandwater.com
Bartholomew website address: www.bartholomewmaps.com
e-mail: roadcheck@harpercollins.co.uk

Mapping generated from Bartholomew digital databases

Printed in Hong Kong   ISBN 0 00 711248 3   Imp 001   OI10795   CDDD

HarperCollinsPublishers

Scale: 9 miles to 1 inch (10 km to 17.5 mm)

0   10   20 miles

0   10   20   30 kilometres

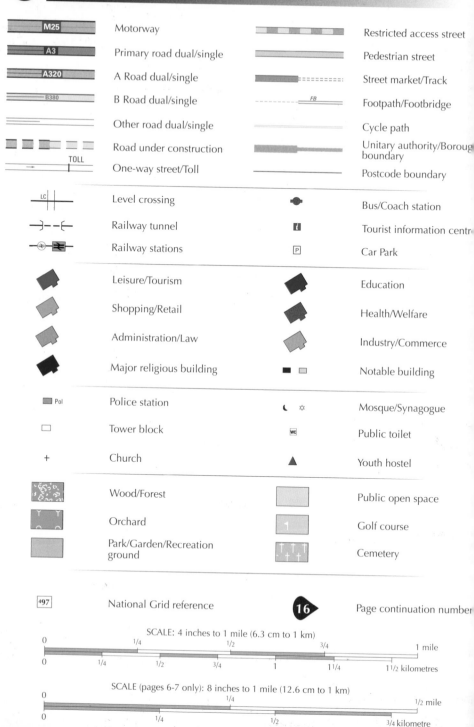

M25	Motorway		Restricted access street
A3	Primary road dual/single		Pedestrian street
A320	A Road dual/single		Street market/Track
B380	B Road dual/single	FB	Footpath/Footbridge
	Other road dual/single		Cycle path
	Road under construction		Unitary authority/Borough boundary
TOLL	One-way street/Toll		Postcode boundary

LC Level crossing

Railway tunnel

Railway stations

Bus/Coach station

Tourist information centre

P Car Park

Leisure/Tourism

Education

Shopping/Retail

Health/Welfare

Administration/Law

Industry/Commerce

Major religious building

Notable building

Pol Police station

Mosque/Synagogue

Tower block

WC Public toilet

+ Church

▲ Youth hostel

Wood/Forest

Public open space

Orchard

Golf course

Park/Garden/Recreation ground

Cemetery

497 National Grid reference

16 Page continuation number

SCALE: 4 inches to 1 mile (6.3 cm to 1 km)

0   1/4   1/2   3/4   1 mile

0   1/4   1/2   3/4   1   1 1/4   1 1/2 kilometres

SCALE (pages 6-7 only): 8 inches to 1 mile (12.6 cm to 1 km)

0   1/4   1/2 mile

0   1/4   1/2   3/4 kilometre

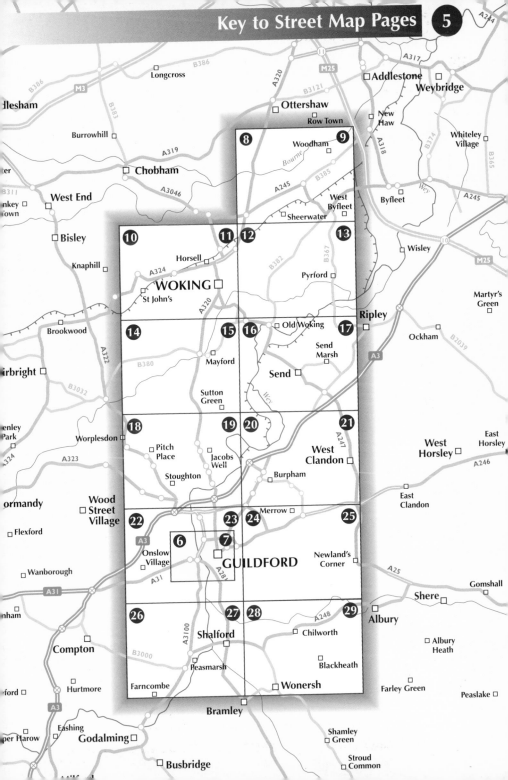

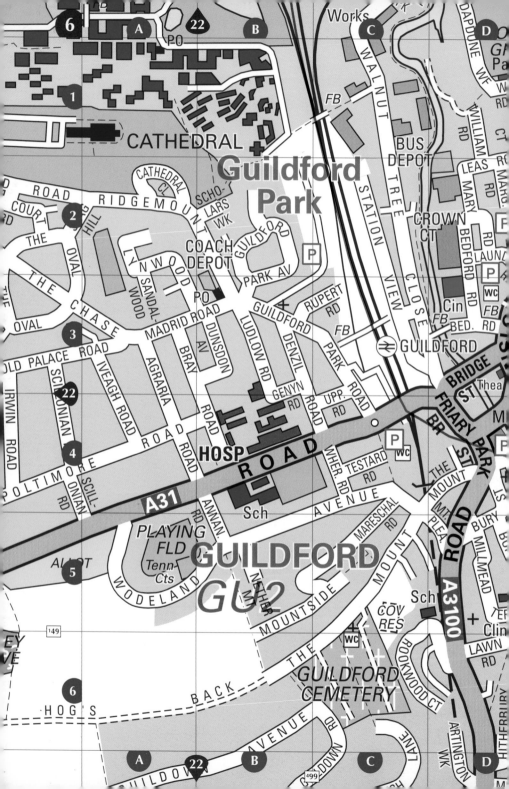

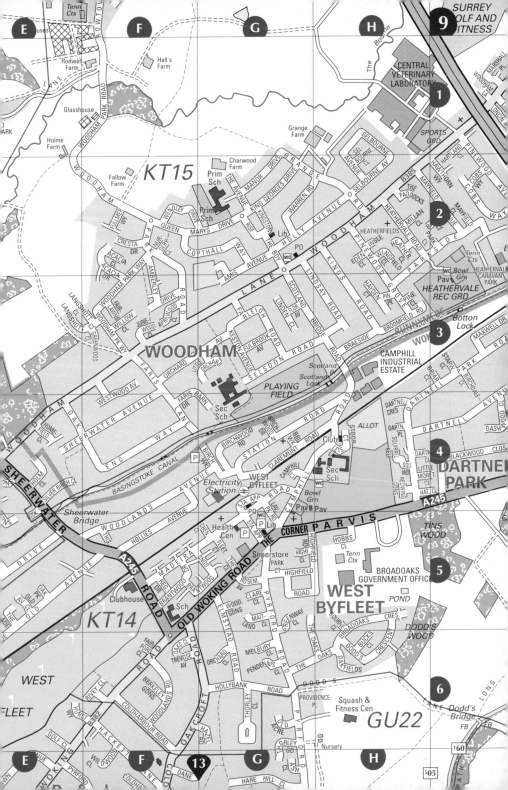

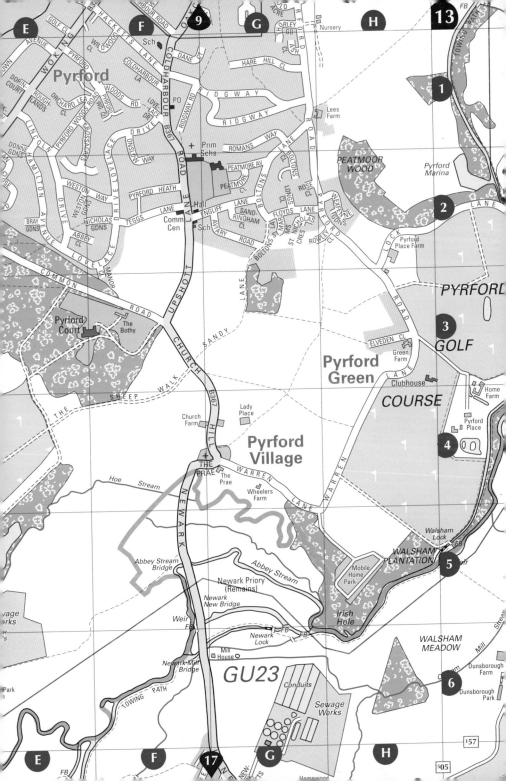

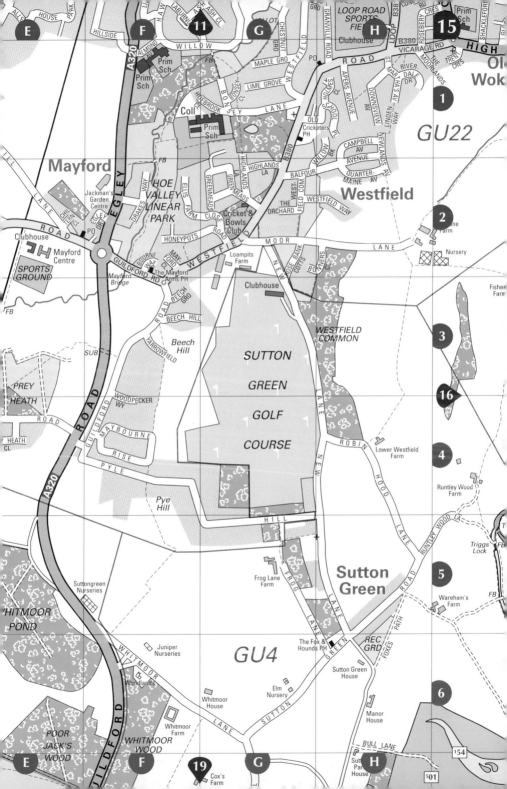

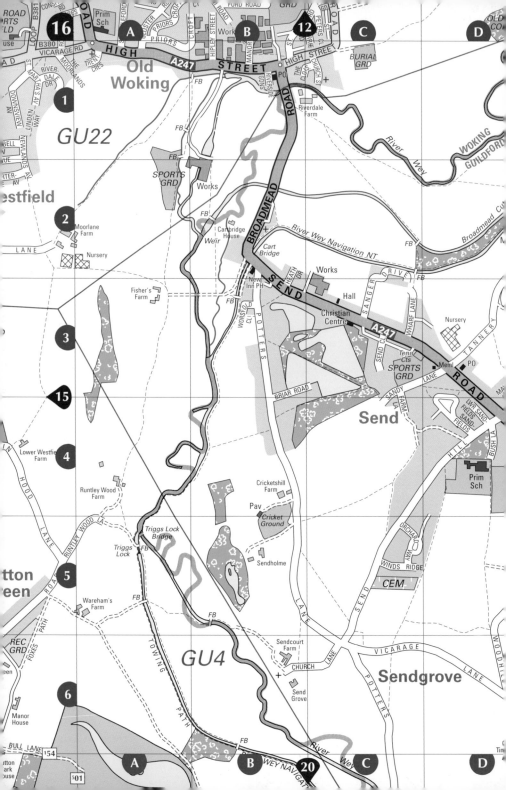

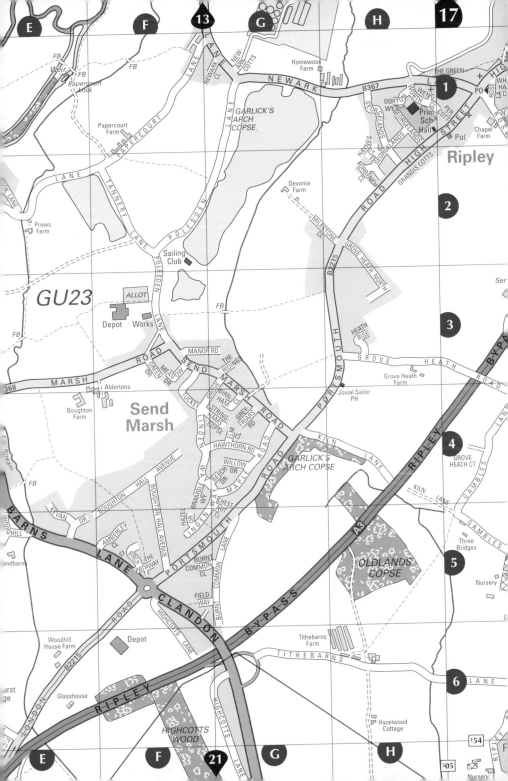

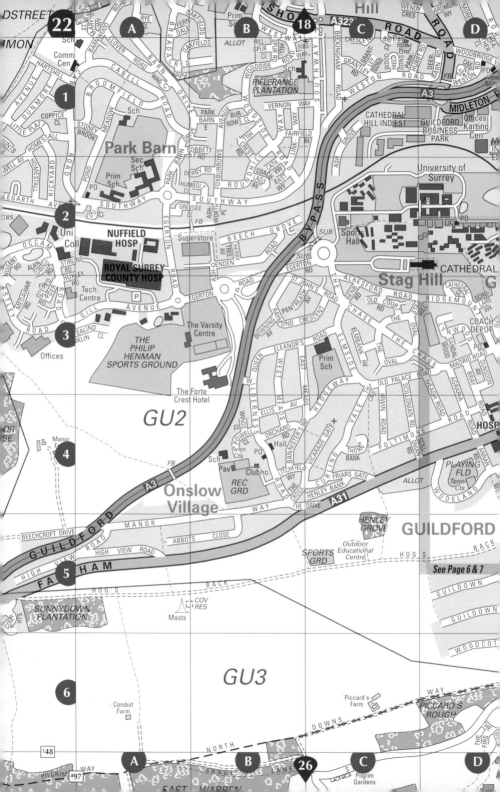

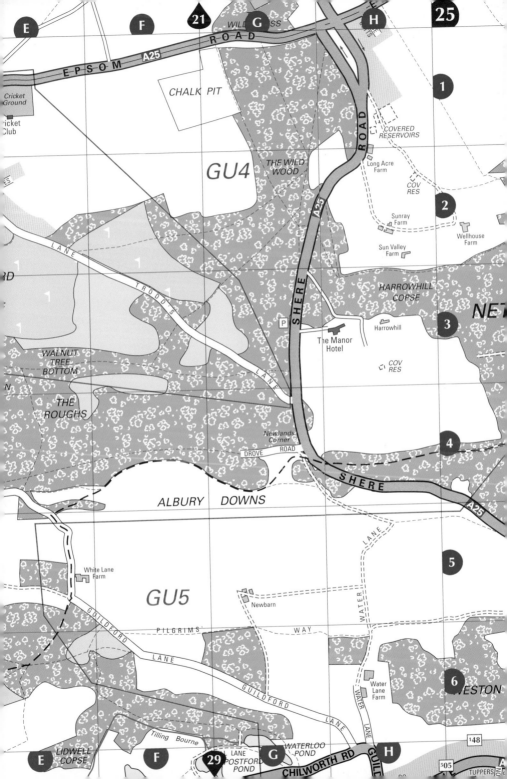

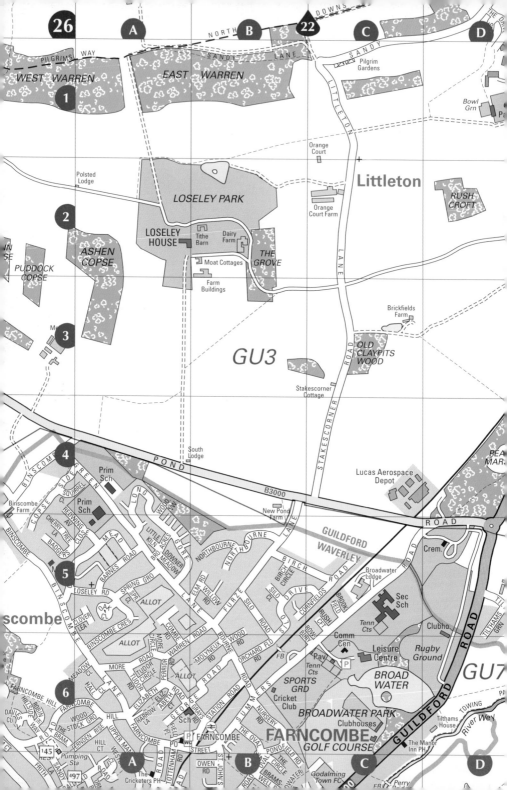

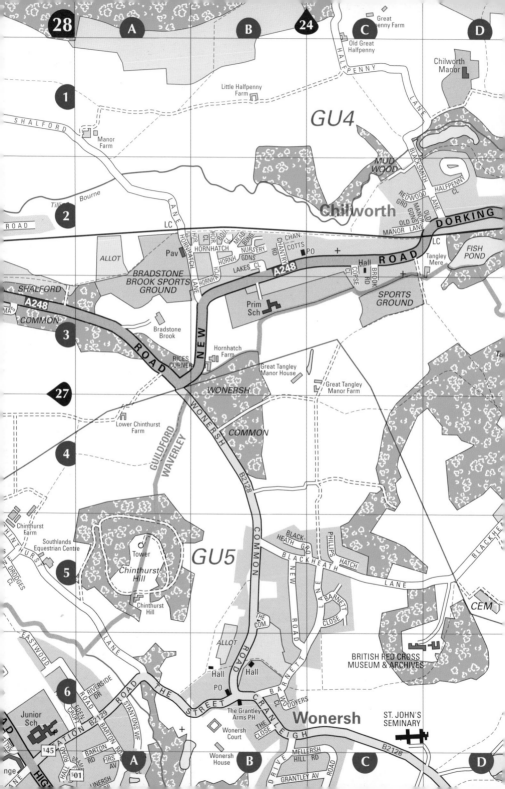

USEFUL INFORMATION

Tourist Information
Guildford Tourist Information Centre, 14 Tunsgate,
Guildford GU1 3QT   *Tel: 01483 444333*   **7 F4**

Woking Visitor Information Centre, Crown House,
Crown Square, Woking GU21 1H   *Tel: 01483 720103*   **11 H3**

Crematorium
Guildford Crematorium, Broadwater, New Pond Road,
Godalming GU7 3DB   *Tel: 01483 444711/ 303976*   **26 D5**

Woking Crematorium, Hermitage Road, St. Johns,
Woking GU21 1TJ   *Tel: 01483 472197*   **10 A5**

Main Library
Guildford Library, 77 North Street, Guildford GU1 4AL
Tel. 01483 568496   **7 F3**

Woking Library, Gloucester Walk, Woking GU21 1EP
Tel: 01483 770591   **11 H3**

Main Post Offices
15 North Street, Guildford GU1 4BB   *Tel: 01483 539181*   **7**
Market Square, Woking GU21 1AA   *Tel: 01483 723973*   **11**

Police
Surrey Police Headquarters
Mount Browne, Sandy Lane, Guildford GU3 1HG
Tel: 01483 571212   Web Site: www.surrey.police.uk   **26 D1**

Guildford Police Station, Margaret Road, Guildford
GU1 4QS   *Tel: 01483 531111*   **6 D2**

Woking Police Station, Station Approach, Woking
GU22 7SY   *Tel: 01483 761991*   **11 H4**

ADMINISTRATION

Guildford Borough Council, Millmead House, Millmead,
Guildford GU2 4BB   *Tel: 01483 505050*
Web Site: www.guildford.gov.uk   **7 E5**

Woking Borough Council, Civic Offices, Gloucester Square,
Woking GU21 1YL
Tel: 01483 755855   www.woking.gov.uk   **11 H3**

FURTHER EDUCATION

University of Surrey, Guildford GU2 7XH
Tel: 01483 300800   Web Site: www.surrey.ac.uk   **22 D2**

Guildford College of Further & Higher Education
Stoke Park, Guildford GU1 1EZ
Tel: 01483 44 85 00   Web Site: www.guildford.ac.uk   **23 F1**

Guildford Area Adult Education, Sydenham Rd
Guildford GU1 3RX   *Tel: 01483 880400*   **7 G3**

Woking College, Rydens Way, Woking GU22 9DL
Tel: 01483 761036   Web Site: www.woking.ac.uk   **12 A6**

ENTERTAINMENT

Cinemas
Ambassadors Cinemas, The Peacocks Centre, Woking
GU21 1GQ   *Tel: 01483 545945*
Web Site: www.theambassadors.com/woking/cinema.html   **11 G3**

Odeon Cinema, Bedford Road, Guildford GU1 3JN
Tel: 0870 5050007   Web Site: www.odeon.co.uk   **6 D3**

Theatres
Electric Theatre, Onslow Street, Guildford GU1 4SZ
Tel: 01483 444 789   Web Site: www.electrictheatre.co.uk   **6 D3**

Guildford Civic, London Road, Guildford GU1 2AA
Tel: 01483 444720   Web Site: www.guildford-civic.co.uk   **7 G2**

New Victoria Theatre, The Ambassadors, Peacocks Centre,
Woking GU21 1GQ   *Tel: 01483 545900*
Web Site: www.theambassadors.com/woking/newvic.html   **11 C**

Rhoda McGaw Theatre, The Ambassadors, Peacocks Centre,
Woking GU21 1GQ   *Tel: 01483 545900*
Web Site: www.theambassadors.com/woking/rhoda.html   **11 G3**

Yvonne Arnaud Theatre, Millbrook, Guildford GU1 3UX
Tel: 01483 440000   Web Site: www.yvonne-arnaud.co.uk   **6 E**

HEALTH

Royal Surrey County Hospital,
Egerton Road, Guildford GU2 5XX
Tel: 01483 571122   A&E Department   **22 A2**

Farnham Road Hospital, Farnham Road, Guildford,
GU2 5XL   *Tel: 01483 443535*   **6 B4**

St. Lukes Hospital, Egerton Road, Guildford GU2 5XX
Tel: 01483 571122   **22 A2**

Woking Community Hospital, Heathside Road, Woking
GU22 7HS   *Tel: 01483 715911*   **11 H4**

Independent Hospitals
Mount Alvernia Hospital, Harvey Road, Guildford GU1 3LX
Tel: 01483 570122   Web Site: www.mtalvernia-hospital.org   **7**

Guildford Nuffield Hospital, Stirling Road, Guildford GU2 7RF
Tel: 01483 555800
Web Site: www.nuffieldhospitals.org.uk   **22 A2**

HELP AND ADVICE

Childline   *Helpline: 0800 1111 Web Site: www.childline.org.uk*

Citizens Advice bureaux   *Web Site: www.nacab.org.uk*
15-21 Haydon Place, Guildford GU1 4LL Tel: 01483 576699 **7 E2**

Provincial House, 26 Commercial Way, Woking GU21 1EN
Tel: 01483 763840 Web Site: www.wokingcab.org.uk   **11 H3**

Missing Persons   *Helpline: 0500 700 7000*
Web Site: www.missingpersons.org

NSPCC   *Helpline: 0808 800500*
Web Site: www.nspcc.org.uk

Rape Crisis Federation   *Helpline: 0115 934 8474*
Web Site: www.rapecrisis.co.uk

CA *Helpline: 0870 444 3127*
Site: www.rspca.org.uk

aritans *Helpline: 08457 909090*
Site: www.samaritans.org.uk
Voodbridge Road, Guildford GU1 4RD
01483 505555 **22 D1**

Victim Support Helpline: 0845 303 0900
Web Site: www.victimsupport.com
PO Box 26 Guildford GU1 4XN Tel: 01483 503173
80A Rydens Way, Woking GU22 9DN Tel: 01483 770457 **12 A6**

DIA

al Newspapers

dford Times *Tel: 01483 579244*

ing Review *Tel: 01483 769991*

ing News & Mail *Tel: 01483 755755*

ing Informer *Tel: 01784 433773*

Local Radio

BBC Southern Counties Radio FM 104.6 MHz
Tel: 01483 306 306
Web Site: www.bbc.co.uk/england/southerncounties

The Eagle FM 96.4 MHz
Tel: 01483 300964 Web Site: www.964eagle.co.uk

County Sound AM 1556 kHz
Tel: 01483 300964 Web Site: www.countysound.co.uk

RT & LEISURE

ure/Sports Centres

dford Spectrum, Parkway, Guildford GU1 1UP
01483 443322
Site: www.guildfordspectrum.co.uk **23 G1**

ston Churchill School Sports Centre, Hermitage Road,
ing GU21 1TL Tel: 01483 797015 **10 B4**

ing High Recreation Centre, Woking High School,
on Road, Woking GU21 4TJ *Tel: 01483 888447* **11 F1**

ing Leisure Centre, Kingfield Road, Woking
2 9BA *Tel: 01483 771122* **11 H5**

ing Planets, Crown Square, Woking GU21 1HR
01483 712710 **11 H3**

nming Pools

dford Lido, Stoke Road, Guildford GU1 1HB
01483 444888 **23 F1**

in the Park, Woking Park, Woking GU22
01483 771122 **11 H5**

Clubs

aley Golf Club, Bramley, Guildford GU5 0AL
01483 893042 **27 G6**

dwater Park Golf Club, Guildford Road, Farncombe,
alming GU7 3BU *Tel: 01483 429955* **26 C6**

don Regis Golf Club, Epsom Road, West Clandon
7TT Tel: 01483 224888 **21 H5**

dford Golf Club, High Path Road, Merrow GU1 2HL
01483 563941 **24 C2**

oridge Golf Centre, Old Woking Road, Old Woking
2 8JH Tel: 01483 722611
Site: www.hoebridge.co.uk **12 C5**

Zealand Golf Club, Woodham Lane, Addlestone
3QD Tel: 01932 345049 **8 D4**

Pyrford Golf Club, Warren Lane, Pyrford GU22 8XR
Tel: 01483 723555 **13 H3**

Sutton Green Golf Club, Sutton Green, Woking GU4 7QF
Tel: 01483 747898 **15 G3**

West Byfleet Golf Club, Sheerwater Road KT14 6AA
Tel: 01932 343433 **9 F5**

Woking Golf Club, Pond Road, Hook Heath, Woking
GU22 0JZ *Tel: 01483 760053* **10 C6**

Worplesdon Golf Club, Heath House Road, Woking
GU22 0RA *Tel: 01483 472277* **14 A2**

Shopping

Friary Shopping Centre, Guildford GU1 4YT
Tel: 01483 503773 **6 D3**

Guildford Market *(Fri - Sat)*, North Street, Guildford GU1
Tel: 01483 444530 **7 E3**

Peacocks Shopping Centre, Victoria Way, Woking GU21 1GB
Tel: 01483 750263 Web Site: www.peacocks-centre.co.uk **11 G3**

Tunsgate Square Shopping Centre, 98-110 High Street,
Guildford GU1 3HE *Tel: 01483 537153*
Web Site: www.tunsgate.co.uk **7 F4**

Woking Market (Mon - Sat), Peacocks Walk, off Commercial Way,
Woking GU21 *Tel: 01483 743208* **11 H3**

Wolsey Place Shopping Centre, Woking GU21 1XX
Tel: 01483 740793/767896 **11 G3**

Shopmobility

The Peacocks Shopping Centre, Victoria Way, Woking GU21 1GD
Tel: 01483 776612/727949
Web Site: www.wokingshopmobility.co.uk **11 G3**

Level 3, Bedford Road Car Park, Guildford GU1 4SA
Tel: 01483 453993 **6 D2**

NSPORT *National Traveline 0870 608 2608*

dford Link (Park & Ride)

gton *(Mon to Sat)* **26 D5**
fford Park Road *(Mon to Sat)* **6 B2**
mead *(Sat only)* **23 F1**
trum *(Mon to Fri)* **23 G1**
ersity *(Sat only)* **22 D2**

Information Tel: 01483 750525
fford Bus Station, The Friary, Guildford GU1 4YP
01483 575226 **6 D3**

er Bus *Tel: 01483 747864*

Guildford Dial-a-Ride *Tel: 01483 444275*

Woking Community Transport *Tel: 01483 747864*

Railway Stations *Information Tel: 08457 484950*

Clandon **21 H3**		Shalford **27 G3**
Farncombe **26 B6**		West Byfleet **9 G4**
Guildford **6 C3**		Woking **11 H3**
London Road **7 G1**		Worplesdon **14 D4**

32 Index to Street Names

General Abbreviations

All	Alley	Conv	Convent	Gdn	Garden	Ms	Mews	Sec	Secondary
Allot	Allotments	Cor	Corner	Gdns	Gardens	Mt	Mount	Shop	Shopping
Amb	Ambulance	Coron	Coroners	Govt	Government	Mus	Museum	Sq	Square
App	Approach	Cors	Corners	Gra	Grange	N	North	St.	Saint
Arc	Arcade	Cotts	Cottages	Grd	Ground	NT	National	St	Street
Av/Ave	Avenue	Cov	Covered	Grds	Grounds		Trust	Sta	Station
Bdy	Broadway	Crem	Crematorium	Grn	Green	Nat	National	Sts	Streets
Bk	Bank	Cres	Crescent	Grns	Greens	PH	Public House	Sub	Subway
Bldgs	Buildings	Ct	Court	Gro	Grove	PO	Post Office	Swim	Swimming
Boul	Boulevard	Cts	Courts	Gros	Groves	Par	Parade	TA	Territorial
Bowl	Bowling	Ctyd	Courtyard	Gt	Great	Pas	Passage		Army
Br/Bri	Bridge	Dep	Depot	Ho	House	Pav	Pavilion	TH	Town Hall
C of E	Church of	Dev	Development	Hos	Houses	Pk	Park	Tenn	Tennis
	England	Dr	Drive	Hosp	Hospital	Pl	Place	Ter	Terrace
Cath	Cathedral	Dws	Dwellings	Hts	Heights	Pol	Police	Thea	Theatre
Cem	Cemetery	E	East	Ind	Industrial	Prec	Precinct	Trd	Trading
Cen	Central,	Ed	Education	Int	International	Prim	Primary	Twr	Tower
	Centre	Elec	Electricity	Junct	Junction	Prom	Promenade	Twrs	Towers
Cft	Croft	Embk	Embankment	La	Lane	Pt	Point	Uni	University
Cfts	Crofts	Est	Estate	Las	Lanes	Quad	Quadrant	Up	Upper
Ch	Church	Ex	Exchange	Lib	Library	RC	Roman	Vil	Villa, Villas
Chyd	Churchyard	Exhib	Exhibition	Lo	Lodge		Catholic	Vw	View
Cin	Cinema	FB	Footbridge	Lwr	Lower	Rd	Road	W	West
Circ	Circus	FC	Football Club	Mag	Magistrates	Rds	Roads	Wd	Wood
Cl/Clo	Close	Fld	Field	Mans	Mansions	Rec	Recreation	Wds	Woods
Co	County	Flds	Fields	Mem	Memorial	Res	Reservoir	Wf	Wharf
Coll	College	Fm	Farm	Mid	Middle	Ri	Rise	Wk	Walk
Comm	Community	Gall	Gallery	Mkt	Market	S	South	Wks	Works
Comn	Common	Gar	Garage	Mkts	Markets	Sch	School	Yd	Yard

District Abbreviations

Add.	Addlestone	Gdmg.	Godalming	W. Byf.	West Byfleet
Cher.	Chertsey	Guil.	Guildford	Wok.	Woking

This index contains streets that are not named on the map due to insufficient space. For each of these cases the nearest street that does appear on the map is also listed in *italics*.

A

Abbey Cl, Wok.	13	E2
Abbey Rd, Wok.	11	E3
Abbot Rd, Guil.	7	F5
Abbots Cl, Guil.	22	A5
Abbots Way, Guil.	24	D1
Abbotsford Cl, Wok.	12	A3
Onslow Cres		
Abbotswood, Guil.	19	H5
Abbotswood Cl, Guil.	19	H5
Abercorn Way, Wok.	10	C4
Abingdon Cl, Wok.	10	D4
Abinger Way, Guil.	20	B3
Acacia Av, Wok.	11	F6
Acacia Cl, Add.	9	F2
Acacia Dr, Add.	9	F2
Acacia Rd, Guil.	23	F2
Achilles Pl, Wok.	11	E3
Acorn Gro, Wok.	15	G1
Old Sch Pl		
Addison Rd, Guil.	7	H3
Addison Rd, Wok.	11	H3
Chertsey Rd		
Admirals Ct, Guil.	24	B1
Agraria Rd, Guil.	6	A3
Ainsdale Way, Wok.	10	C4
Albert Dr, Wok.	8	D6
Albion Ho, Wok.	11	H3
Albury Rd, Guil.	23	H3
Aldersey Rd, Guil.	23	H2
Aldershot Rd, Guil.	18	B6
Alexandra Pl, Guil.	23	H4
Alexandra Ter, Guil.	7	G3
Alford Cl, Guil.	19	H5
Alice Ruston Pl, Wok.	11	E5
Alison Cl, Wok.	11	G1
Allen Ho Pk, Wok.	11	E6
Allingham Ct, Gdmg.	26	B6
Summers Rd		
Alloway Cl, Wok.	10	D4
Inglewood		
Alma Cl, Wok.	10	A4
Almond Av, Wok.	15	F1
Almond Cl, Guil.	19	F4
Alpha Rd, Wok.	12	B2
Alresford Rd, Guil.	22	C3
Alterton Cl, Wok.	10	C3
Alwyne Ct, Wok.	11	G2
Amberley Cl, Wok.	17	F5
Amberley Dr, Add.	9	F2
Amis Av, Add.	9	G3
Amis Rd, Wok.	10	A5
Amstel Way, Wok.	10	B4
Angel Gate, Guil.	7	E3
High St		
Angelica Rd, Guil.	18	C4
Annandale Rd, Guil.	6	B4
Anston Ct, Guil.	22	A2
Southway		
Anthonys, Wok.	8	B4
Apers Av, Wok.	15	H1
Apollo Pl, Wok.	10	C5
Church Rd		
Appletree Ct, Guil.	20	D5
Old Merrow St		
Aprilwood Cl, Add.	9	F3
Ardmore Av, Guil.	18	D6
Ardmore Way, Guil.	18	D6
Armadale Rd, Wok.	10	C3
Arnold Rd, Wok.	12	B2
Arthur's Br Rd, Wok.	11	E3
Artillery Rd, Guil.	7	E2
Artillery Ter, Guil.	7	E1
Artington Wk, Guil.	6	D6
Ash Cl, Wok.	11	G6
Ash Cl (Pyrford), Wok.	13	G1
Ash Gro, Guil.	22	C2
Ash Rd, Wok.	11	F6
Ashbury Cres, Guil.	20	C6
Ashcroft, Guil.	27	G3
Ashenden Rd, Guil.	22	B3
Ashley Ct, Wok.	10	B4
Ashley Gdns, Guil.	27	H3
Ashley Rd, Wok.	10	B4
Ashton Rd, Wok.	10	B3
Ashwindham Ct, Wok.	10	A4
Ashwood Pk, Wok.	12	A4
Ashwood Rd, Wok.	11	H4
Ashworth Pl, Guil.	22	B2
Aspen Cl, Guil.	20	D5
Atherton Cl, Guil.	27	G2
Atkins Cl, Wok.	10	C4
Greythorne Rd		
Austen Rd, Guil.	23	H3
Avenue, The, Add.	9	G2
Avenue, The, Guil.	18	A1
Aviary Rd, Wok.	13	G2
Avington Cl, Guil.	7	H1
London Rd		
Avonmead, Wok.	11	E4
Silversmiths Way		
Avonmore Av, Guil.	23	H1
Azalea Ct, Wok.	11	F5

B

B.A.T. Export Ho, Wok.	11	G3
Baden Rd, Guil.	18	D6
Badger Cl, Guil.	18	D5
Badgers Cl, Wok.	11	E4
Baillie Rd, Guil.	23	H3
Bainton Mead, Wok.	10	C3
Baldwin Cres, Guil.	20	C6
Balfour Av, Wok.	15	G2
Balmoral Dr, Wok.	12	C2
Bampton Way, Wok.	10	C4
Banders Ri, Guil.	24	C1
Banks Way, Guil.	19	H5
Bankside, Wok.	10	D4
Wyndham Rd		
Bannister's Rd, Guil.	22	B4
Bardon Wk, Wok.	10	D3
Bampton Way		
Bargate Ct, Guil.	22	A2
Park Barn Dr		
Barnard Ct, Wok.	10	A4
Raglan Rd		
Barnes Rd, Gdmg.	26	A5
Barnett Cl, Guil.	28	C5
Barnett La, Guil.	28	B6
Barnett Row, Guil.	19	F3
Barnwood Cl, Guil.	18	A6
Barnwood Rd, Guil.	22	A1
Barrack Path, Wok.	10	B4
Barrack Rd, Guil.	18	C6
Barrens Brae, Wok.	12	A4
Barrens Cl, Wok.	12	A4
Barrens Pk, Wok.	12	A4
Barricane, Wok.	10	D5
Bars, The, Guil.	7	E2
Barton Rd, Guil.	28	A6
Basset Cl, Add.	9	H2
Bassett Rd, Wok.	12	C2
Bateson Way, Wok.	8	C6
Batten Av, Wok.	10	A5
Bayliss Ct, Guil.	6	D2
Mary Rd		
Beacon Hill, Wok.	11	E4
Beaconsfield Rd, Wok.	11	H6
Beatty Av, Guil.	24	A1

Beaufort Cl, Wok.	12	C2
Beaufort Rd, Wok.	12	C2
Beavers Cl, Guil.	22	A1
Beckingham Rd, Guil.	18	C6
Bedford Cl, Wok.	11	E1
Bedford Rd, Guil.	6	D2
Bedser Cl, Wok.	12	A2
Beech Dr, Wok.	17	G4
Beech Gdns, Wok.	11	G1
Beech Gro, Guil.	22	B2
Beech Gro, Wok.	15	F3
Beech Hill, Wok.	15	F3
Beech La, Guil.	23	E5
Beech Lawn, Guil.	23	H3
Beech Vale, Wok.	11	H4
Hill Vw Rd		
Beeches, The, Guil.	27	H6
Beechway, Guil.	24	B1
Beechwood Cl, Wok.	10	A3
Beechwood Rd, Wok.	10	A3
Belgrave Manor, Wok.	11	G5
Bellfields Ct, Guil.	19	E4
Oak Tree Dr		
Bellfields Rd, Guil.	19	F6
Belmont Av, Guil.	18	B5
Belmore Av, Wok.	12	D2
Belvedere Cl, Guil.	18	D6
Benbrick Rd, Guil.	22	C3
Bennett Way, Guil.	21	G3
Bentham Av, Wok.	12	C1
Berberis Cl, Guil.	19	E6
Berkeley Gdns, W.Byf.	9	F6
Berkley Ct, Guil.	7	H1
London Rd		
Beta Rd, Wok.	12	B2
Bingham Dr, Wok.	10	B4
Binscombe Cres, Gdmg.	26	A6
Birch Circle, Gdmg.	26	B5
Birch Cl, Wok.	11	E5
Birch Cl (Send Marsh), Wok.	17	F5
Birch Gro, Wok.	12	D1
Birch Rd, Gdmg.	26	B5
Birch Wk, W.Byf.	9	G4
Birches, The, Wok.	11	H4
Heathside Rd		
Birchwood Dr, W.Byf.	9	G4
Birchwood Rd, W.Byf.	9	G4
Birdswood Dr, Wok.	10	A5
Birnham Cl, Wok.	17	G3
Bishops Wd, Wok.	10	B3
Bitterne Dr, Wok.	10	B3
Blackberry Cl, Guil.	18	D5
Blackbridge Rd, Wok.	11	F5
Blackdown Av, Wok.	13	E1
Blackdown Cl, Wok.	12	C2
Blackheath Gro, Guil.	28	B5
Blackheath La, Guil.	29	H2
Blackmore Cres, Wok.	12	B1
Blackness La, Wok.	11	G5
Blacksmith La, Guil.	28	C1
Bladon Cl, Guil.	24	A1
Blanchards Hill, Guil.	19	G2
Blandford Cl, Wok.	12	B3
Blencarn Cl, Wok.	10	B2
Blenheim Cl, W.Byf.	9	F5
Madeira Rd		
Blenheim Gdns, Wok.	10	D5
Bloomfield Cl, Wok.	10	A4
Bloomsbury Ct, Guil.	23	H3
St. Lukes Sq		
Bluebell Ct, Wok.	11	F5
Board Sch Rd, Wok.	11	H2
Boltons Cl, Wok.	13	G2
Boltons La, Wok.	13	G2
Bonners Cl, Wok.	15	G2
Bonsey Cl, Wok.	15	G1
Bonsey La, Wok.	15	G1
Boughton Hall Av, Wok.	17	F4
Boundary Rd, Wok.	12	A2
Boundary Way, Wok.	12	A1
Boundary Yd, Wok.	12	A2
Boundary Rd		
Bourne Cl, Guil.	28	B2
Bourne Cl, W.Byf.	9	H5
Bourne Rd, Gdmg.	26	B5
Bourne Way, Wok.	15	F2
Bower Ct, Wok.	12	B2
Princess Rd		
Bowers Cl, Guil.	20	A4
Cotts Wd Dr		
Bowers Fm Dr, Guil.	20	A4
Bowers La, Guil.	20	A3
Boxgrove Av, Guil.	20	A6
Boxgrove La, Guil.	24	A1
Boxgrove Rd, Guil.	24	A1
Bracken Cl, Wok.	11	H4
Bracken Way, Guil.	18	A6
Brackendene Cl, Wok.	12	A1
Bradfield Cl, Guil.	20	A5

Bradfield Cl, Wok.	11	G4
Braeside, Add.	9	H3
Bramble Cl, Guil.	18	A6
Bramble Way, Wok.	17	F4
Brambledene Cl, Wok.	11	E4
Brantwood Cl, W.Byf.	9	G5
Brantwood Gdns		
Brantwood Ct, W.Byf.	9	F5
Brantwood Dr		
Brantwood Dr, W.Byf.	9	F5
Brantwood Gdns,	9	F5
W.Byf.		
Bray Gdns, Wok.	13	E2
Bray Rd, Guil.	6	A3
Brewery Rd, Wok.	11	F3
Briar Rd, Wok.	16	B3
Briar Wk, W.Byf.	9	G4
Briar Way, Guil.	20	B4
Bridge Barn La, Wok.	11	E3
Bridge Cl, Wok.	11	E3
Bridge Ct, Wok.	11	F3
Bridge Ms, Wok.	11	F3
Bridge Barn La		
Bridge Pk, Guil.	20	C5
Bridge St, Guil.	6	D3
Bridgehill Cl, Guil.	22	C1
Brierly Cl, Guil.	18	C6
Bright Hill, Guil.	7	F4
Brittens Cl, Guil.	18	C3
Broad Acres, Gdmg.	26	A5
Broadacres, Guil.	18	A6
Broadford Pk, Guil.	27	F3
Broadford Rd, Guil.	27	E4
Broadmead Rd, Wok.	16	B2
Broadmeads, Wok.	16	B2
Broadmead		
Broadoaks Cres, W.Byf.	9	H6
Broadwater Cl, Wok.	8	D4
Broadwater Ri, Guil.	24	A2
Broadway, The, Add.	9	G2
Broadway, The, Wok.	11	H3
Brockway Cl, Guil.	20	B6
Brodie Rd, Guil.	7	G3
Broke Ct, Guil.	20	C5
Speedwell Cl		
Brook La, Wok.	17	E2
Brook Rd, Guil.	28	C2
Brookfield, Gdmg.	26	C5
Brookfield, Wok.	10	D2
Brooklyn Cl, Wok.	11	G5
Brooklyn Ct, Wok.	11	G5
Brooklyn Rd		
Brooklyn Rd, Wok.	11	G4
Brookside, Guil.	19	F3
Broomcroft Cl, Wok.	12	D2
Broomcroft Dr, Wok.	12	D1
Broomfield, Guil.	22	A1
Broomfield Cl, Guil.	18	A6
Broomfield Rd, Add.	9	H3
Broomhall End, Wok.	11	G2
Broomhall La		
Broomhall La, Wok.	11	G2
Broomhall Rd, Wok.	11	G2
Brox La, Cher.	8	D1
Bryanstone Av, Guil.	18	C5
Bryanstone Cl, Guil.	18	B5
Bryanstone Gro, Guil.	18	B4
Brynford Cl, Wok.	11	G1
Bryony Rd, Guil.	20	B5
Buckingham Cl, Guil.	23	H1
Bucks Cl, W.Byf.	9	H6
Bull La, Guil.	15	H6
Bullbeggars La, Wok.	10	D2
Bunyard Dr, Wok.	8	C6
Burden Way, Guil.	18	D3
Burdenshot Hill, Guil.	14	C5
Burdenshott Rd, Guil.	14	C5
Burdenshott Rd, Wok.	14	C5
Burlingham Cl, Guil.	20	D6
Gilliat Dr		
Burnet Av, Guil.	20	B5
Burnt Common Cl, Wok.	17	F5
Burnt Common La, Wok.	17	G5
Burpham La, Guil.	20	A3
Burrows Cl, Guil.	22	B1
Burwood Cl, Guil.	24	D1
Bury Cl, Wok.	11	F2
Bury Flds, Guil.	6	D5
Bury La, Wok.	11	E2
Bury St, Guil.	6	D5
Bush La, Wok.	16	D4
Bushy Hill Dr, Guil.	20	B6
Butts Rd, Wok.	11	G3
Bylands, Wok.	12	A5
Byrefield Rd, Guil.	18	B5
Byron Cl, Wok.	10	A3

C

Cabell Rd, Guil.	22	A1

Caledon Pl, Guil.	20	A5
Darfield Rd		
Calluna Ct, Wok.	11	H4
Heathside Rd		
Cambridge Cl, Wok.	10	B4
Bingham Dr		
Campbell Av, Wok.	15	H1
Camphill Ct, W.Byf.	9	G4
Camphill Ind Est, W.Byf.	9	H3
Camphill Rd, W.Byf.	9	G4
Candlerush Cl, Wok.	12	B3
Canewdon Cl, Wok.	11	G5
Guildford Rd		
Canterbury Rd, Guil.	18	B6
Capstan's Wf, Wok.	10	B4
Caradon Cl, Wok.	10	D4
Caraway Pl, Guil.	18	C3
Cardamom Cl, Guil.	18	C4
Cardigan Rd, Wok.	10	A4
Bingham Dr		
Cardingham, Wok.	10	C3
Cardwells Keep, Guil.	18	C5
Carlton Rd, Wok.	8	A6
Carmel Cl, Wok.	11	G4
Carolyn Cl, Wok.	10	B5
Carroll Av, Guil.	24	B2
Cartbridge Cl, Wok.	16	B3
Send Rd		
Carters La, Wok.	12	C6
Castle Hill, Guil.	7	E5
Castle Sq, Guil.	7	F4
Castle St, Guil.	7	E4
Catalpa Cl, Guil.	19	E6
Cedar Way		
Cater Gdns, Guil.	18	B6
Cathedral Cl, Guil.	6	A2
Cathedral Hill Ind Est, Guil.	22	C1
Cathedral Vw, Guil.	22	B2
Causeway Ct, Wok.	10	B4
Bingham Dr		
Cavendish Rd, Wok.	11	F5
Cavenham Cl, Wok.	11	G5
Cawsey Way, Wok.	11	G3
Caxton Gdns, Guil.	22	D1
Caxtons Ct, Guil.	20	A6
Cedar Gdns, Wok.	10	D4
Cedar Rd, Wok.	10	D6
St. John's Rd		
Cedar Way, Guil.	19	E6
Cedars, The, Guil.	20	A5
Channings, Wok.	11	G1
Chantry Cotts, Guil.	28	B2
Chantry Rd, Guil.	28	B2
Chantry Vw Rd, Guil.	23	F5
Chapel St, Guil.	7	E4
Castle St		
Chapel St, Wok.	11	H3
Chapelhouse Cl, Guil.	22	A2
Park Barn Dr		
Charlock Way, Guil.	20	B5
Chase, The, Guil.	22	C3
Chasefield Cl, Guil.	20	A5
Chatfield Dr, Guil.	20	C6
Kingfisher Dr		
Chaucer Ct, Guil.	6	D6
Lawn Rd		
Cheniston Cl, W.Byf.	9	G5
Chequer Tree Cl, Wok.	10	A2
Cherry St, Wok.	11	G4
Cherry Tree Av, Guil.	22	B2
Chertsey Rd, Wok.	8	A5
Chertsey St, Guil.	7	F2
Cheselden Rd, Guil.	7	G3
Chesham Ms, Guil.	23	H3
Chesham Rd		
Chesham Rd, Guil.	7	H3
Chester Cl, Wok.	18	B6
Chestnut Av, Guil.	23	E6
Chestnut Cl, Wok.	17	G4
Chestnut Gro, Wok.	11	G6
Chestnut Rd, Guil.	23	F2
Chiltern Cl, Wok.	15	E2
Chilworth Rd, Guil.	29	G1
Chinthurst La, Guil.	27	G3
Chinthurst Pk, Guil.	27	G4
Chipstead Ct, Wok.	10	A3
Creston Av		
Chirton Wk, Guil.	10	C4
Shilburn Way		
Chitty's Common, Guil.	18	B4
Chittys Wk, Guil.	18	B4
Chobham Rd, Wok.	11	G2
Choir Grn, Wok.	10	A3
Semper Cl		
Christchurch Way, Wok.	11	H3
Church St E		
Christie Cl, Guil.	19	F5
Christmas Hill, Guil.	27	H3
Church Cl, Wok.	11	F2

Name	Page	Grid
Church Hill (Horsell), Wok.	11	F2
Church Hill (Pyrford), Wok.	13	F3
Church La, Guil.	29	H1
Church La (Worplesdon), Guil.	18	A1
Church La (Send), Wok.	16	B6
Church Path, Wok.	11	H3
High St		
Church Rd, Guil.	7	E2
Church Rd (Horsell), Wok.	11	G2
Church Rd (Saint John's), Wok.	10	C5
Church St (Old Woking), Wok.	16	C1
Church St E, Wok.	11	H3
Church St W, Wok.	11	G3
Churchfields, Guil.	20	A4
Burpham La		
Churchfields, Wok.	11	G2
Churchill Rd, Guil.	7	H2
Cinder Path, Wok.	11	E5
Cinnamon Gdns, Guil.	18	C3
Clandon Pk, Guil.	21	G6
Clandon Rd, Guil.	7	H2
Clandon Rd (West Clandon), Guil.	17	F5
Clandon Rd, Wok.	17	F5
Clandon Way, Wok.	17	F5
Clandon Rd		
Clare Cl, W.Byf.	9	G5
Claredale, Wok.	11	G5
Claremont Av		
Claremont Av, Wok.	11	G5
Claremont Dr, Wok.	11	G5
Claremont Rd, W.Byf.	9	G4
Clay La, Guil.	19	G2
Claydon Rd, Wok.	10	C2
Clayhanger, Guil.	20	C6
Kingfisher Dr		
Clayton Dr, Guil.	18	B5
Cleardown, Wok.	12	B4
Cleeve, The, Guil.	24	A2
Clifford Manor Rd, Guil.	23	G6
Clifton Way, Wok.	10	B3
Cline Rd, Guil.	23	H4
Cloisters, The, Wok.	16	B1
Close, The, Guil.	28	B6
Close, The, W.Byf.	9	G5
Clover Ct, Wok.	11	F4
Clover Lea, Gdmg.	26	A5
Clover Rd, Guil.	18	A6
Coachlads Av, Guil.	22	B2
Cobbett Rd, Guil.	22	A1
Cobbetts Cl, Wok.	10	D3
Codrington Ct, Wok.	10	A4
Raglan Rd		
Colburn Cres, Guil.	20	A5
Sutherland Dr		
Coldharbour La, Wok.	13	F1
Coldharbour Rd, W.Byf.	9	F6
Coldharbour Rd, Wok.	13	F1
Coley Av, Wok.	12	A4
College La, Wok.	11	E5
College Rd, Guil.	7	E2
College Rd, Wok.	12	B2
Collier Way, Guil.	20	D6
Colliers Cl, Wok.	10	D3
Collingwood Cres, Guil.	24	A1
Coltsfoot Dr, Guil.	20	A5
Colyton Cl, Wok.	11	E4
Combe Rd, Gdmg.	26	A5
Comeragh Cl, Wok.	10	C6
Commercial Rd, Guil.	7	E3
Commercial Way, Wok.	11	H3
Common, The, Guil.	27	G3
Common, The (Wonersh), Guil.	28	B5
Condor Ct, Guil.	6	D5
Millmead Ter		
Conford Dr, Guil.	27	G3
Coniers Way, Guil.	20	B5
Conista Ct, Wok.	10	B2
Roundthorn Way		
Coniston Rd, Wok.	12	B6
Constitution Hill, Wok.	11	G5
Cooper Rd, Guil.	7	H4
Copley Cl, Wok.	10	A5
Copper Beech Cl, Wok.	14	D1
Coppice End, Wok.	13	E2
Copse Cl, Guil.	28	C2
Copse Rd, Wok.	10	B4
Copthall Way, Add.	9	F2
Coriander Cres, Guil.	18	C3
Corner, The, W.Byf.	9	G5
Cornfields, Gdmg.	26	B5
Corrie Rd, Wok.	12	C6
Cotts Wd Dr, Guil.	20	A3
Court Grn Hts, Wok.	11	E6
Courtenay Rd, Wok.	12	A2
Cowslip La, Wok.	10	D1
Craigmore Twr, Wok.	11	G5
Guildford Rd		
Cranfield Ct, Wok.	10	C4
Martindale Rd		
Cranleigh Rd, Guil.	28	B6
Cranley Cl, Guil.	24	A2
Cranley Rd, Guil.	23	H2
Cranstoun Cl, Guil.	18	B4
Crescent, The, Guil.	18	C6
Cresta Dr, Add.	9	F2
Creston Av, Wok.	10	A2
Cross Las, Guil.	7	H1
Crossacres, Wok.	13	E1
Crossways, The, Guil.	22	C3
Crown Hts, Guil.	23	G5
Crown Sq, Wok.	11	H3
Commercial Way		
Cumberland Av, Guil.	18	C3
Cunningham Av, Guil.	24	A1
Curlew Gdns, Guil.	20	D6
Curling Vale, Guil.	22	C4
Cygnet Cl, Wok.	10	D2
Cypress Rd, Guil.	19	E6

D

Name	Page	Grid
Dagden Rd, Guil.	27	G2
Dagley Fm Pk Homes, Guil.	27	F2
Dagley La, Guil.	27	F2
Dairyman's Wk, Guil.	20	B3
Dale Vw, Wok.	10	C4
Dane Ct, Wok.	13	F1
Danes Hill, Wok.	12	A4
Danesrood, Guil.	23	H3
Lower Edgeborough Rd		
Danses Cl, Guil.	20	D6
Dapdune Ct, Guil.	6	D1
Dapdune Rd, Guil.	7	E1
Dapdune Wf, Guil.	23	E2
Darfield Rd, Guil.	20	A5
Dartmouth Av, Wok.	8	C6
Dartmouth Grn, Wok.	8	D6
Dartmouth Path, Wok.	8	D6
Dartnell Av, W.Byf.	9	H4
Dartnell Cl, W.Byf.	9	H4
Dartnell Cres, W.Byf.	9	H4
Dartnell Pl, W.Byf.	9	H4
Darvel Cl, Wok.	10	C2
Darwin Ct, Guil.	19	F4
Daryngton Dr, Guil.	24	B2
Davos Cl, Wok.	11	G5
Dayspring, Guil.	18	D4
De Lara Way, Wok.	11	F4
Deacon Fld, Guil.	22	D1
Midleton Rd		
Dean Cl, Wok.	13	E1
Dedswell Dr, Guil.	21	G2
Deeprose Cl, Guil.	18	D4
Deerbarn Rd, Guil.	22	D1
Dell, The, Wok.	11	E4
Delta Rd, Wok.	12	A2
Dene Cl, Guil.	20	B6
Dene Pl, Wok.	10	D4
Dene Rd, Guil.	7	G2
Denholm Gdns, Guil.	20	A5
Denmark Rd, Guil.	7	G2
Dennis Way, Guil.	19	G3
Denton Way, Wok.	10	B4
Denvale Wk, Wok.	10	C4
Denzil Rd, Guil.	6	B3
Derby Rd, Guil.	22	A2
Derrydown, Wok.	15	E1
Devoil Cl, Guil.	20	B4
Devon Bk, Guil.	6	D6
Portsmouth Rd		
Devonshire Av, Wok.	8	C6
Dianthus Ct, Wok.	11	F4
Dinsdale Cl, Wok.	12	A4
Dodd's Cres, W.Byf.	9	H6
Dodd's La, Wok.	9	G6
Donne Gdns, Wok.	13	E1
Dorchester Ct, Wok.	12	A2
Dorincourt, Wok.	13	E1
Dorking Rd, Wok.	29	F1
Dorrit Cres, Guil.	18	A6
Dorset Dr, Wok.	12	B3
Dorton Way, Wok.	17	H1
Douglas Cl, Guil.	19	F2
Dovedale Cl, Guil.	20	A5
Weylea Av		
Doverfield Rd, Guil.	20	A5
Doversmead, Wok.	10	A2
Down Rd, Guil.	24	B2
Downer Meadow, Gdmg.	26	A5
Downing Av, Guil.	22	B3
Downside Orchard, Wok.	12	A3
Park Rd		
Downside Rd, Guil.	24	B3
Downsview Av, Wok.	15	H1
Downsview Ct, Guil.	19	E4
Hazel Av		
Downsway, Guil.	24	D2

Name	Page	Grid
Drakes Way, Wok.	15	F2
Dray Ct, Guil.	6	A3
The Chase		
Drive, The, Guil.	22	B2
Beech Gro		
Drive, The (Artington), Guil.	22	D6
Drive, The (Onslow Village), Guil.	22	B4
Drive, The, Wok.	10	D6
Drodges Cl, Guil.	27	H5
Drove Rd, Guil.	25	G4
Drummond Rd, Guil.	7	E1
Duke St, Wok.	11	H3
Dukes Ct, Wok.	11	H3
Duncan Dr, Guil.	24	A1
Dunlin Ri, Guil.	20	D6
Dunnets, Wok.	10	A3
Dunsdon Av, Guil.	6	B3
Durham Cl, Guil.	18	B6
Dykes Path, Wok.	12	C1
Bentham Av		

E

Name	Page	Grid
Eagle Rd, Guil.	7	F1
Easington Pl, Guil.	23	H3
Maori Rd		
East Gdns, Wok.	12	C3
East Hill, Wok.	12	C2
East Meads, Guil.	22	B3
East Shalford La, Guil.	27	G1
East Way, Guil.	22	B2
Eastbrook Cl, Wok.	12	A2
Eastgate Gdns, Guil.	7	G2
Eastmead, Wok.	10	D3
Eastwood Rd, Guil.	27	H6
Eaton Rd, Guil.	20	A6
Echo Pit Rd, Guil.	23	G6
Ecob Cl, Guil.	18	B4
Eden Cl, Add.	9	H2
Edencroft, Guil.	27	H6
Effingham Ct, Wok.	11	G4
Constitution Hill		
Egerton Ct, Guil.	22	A2
Egerton Rd		
Egerton Rd, Guil.	22	A2
Egley Dr, Wok.	15	F2
Egley Rd, Wok.	15	F2
Elder Cl, Guil.	20	A5
Elgin Gdns, Guil.	24	A1
Elizabeth Ct, Gdmg.	26	A6
Elizabeth Rd, Gdmg.	26	A6
Elkins Gdns, Guil.	20	A5
Elles Av, Guil.	24	B2
Ellis Av, Guil.	22	B4
Ellis Fm Cl, Wok.	15	F2
Elm Cl, Wok.	11	F1
Elm Cl (Send Marsh), Wok.	17	G4
Elm Rd, Gdmg.	26	B5
Elm Rd, Wok.	11	F4
Elm Rd (Horsell), Wok.	11	H1
Elmbank Av, Guil.	22	C3
Elmbridge La, Wok.	11	H5
Elmdene, Wok.	11	G4
Constitution Hill		
Elmhurst Ct, Guil.	23	H3
Lower Edgeborough Rd		
Elmside, Guil.	22	C3
Elmstead Rd, W.Byf.	9	G5
Elsdon Rd, Wok.	10	C3
Elveden Cl, Wok.	13	H3
Ely Pl, Guil.	18	B6
Canterbury Rd		
Emmanuel Cl, Guil.	18	C5
Emmetts Cl, Wok.	11	E3
Engliff La, Wok.	13	F2
Ennismore Av, Guil.	23	H2
Epsom Rd, Guil.	7	H3
Erica Ct, Wok.	11	F4
Escombe Dr, Guil.	18	D3
Europa Pk Rd, Guil.	23	E1
Eustace Rd, Guil.	20	D6
Eve Rd, Wok.	12	B1
Evelyn Cl, Wok.	11	F6
Everest Ct, Wok.	10	A2
Langmans Way		
Everlands Ct, Wok.	11	G4
Exeter Pl, Guil.	18	B6

F

Name	Page	Grid
Fairborne Way, Guil.	18	C5
Fairbourne Cl, Wok.	10	C4
Abercorn Way		
Fairfax Rd, Guil.	12	B6
Fairfield Ri, Guil.	22	B1
Fairford Cl, W.Byf.	9	G4
Fairlawns, Add.	9	F3
Fairmead, Wok.	11	E4
Fairview Av, Wok.	11	G4

Name	Page	Grid
Fairview Cl, Wok.	11	H4
Fairview Av		
Fairway, Guil.	24	D1
Fairway Cl, Wok.	10	C5
Falcon Ct, Wok.	8	C6
Blackmore Cres		
Falcon Rd, Guil.	7	F1
Falstone, Wok.	10	D4
Faris Barn Dr, Add.	9	F4
Faris La, Add.	9	F3
Farleigh Ct, Guil.	22	A2
Park Barn Dr		
Farleigh Rd, Add.	9	G3
Farm Cl, Guil.	19	F5
Christie Cl		
Farm La, Wok.	16	C4
Farm Rd, Wok.	12	B6
Farm Wk, Guil.	22	B4
Wilderness Rd		
Farmhouse Cl, Wok.	12	D1
Farncombe St, Gdmg.	26	A6
Farnley, Wok.	10	B3
Farthings, Wok.	10	A2
Felix Dr, Guil.	21	G2
Fennel Cl, Guil.	20	B5
Fenns Way, Wok.	11	G1
Fentum Rd, Guil.	18	C6
Fenwick Cl, Wok.	10	D4
Ferndale, Guil.	18	A6
Ferndale Rd, Wok.	11	H2
Ferndown Cl, Guil.	24	A3
Ferndown Ct, Guil.	23	E1
Fernhill Cl, Wok.	11	E6
Fernhill La, Wok.	11	E6
Fernhill Pk, Wok.	11	E6
Ferry La, Guil.	23	E6
Portsmouth Rd		
Festival Path, Wok.	10	B5
Field Cl, Guil.	20	D6
Field La, Guil.	26	B6
The Oval		
Field Pl, Gdmg.	26	A6
Field Way, Wok.	17	F5
Fielders Grn, Guil.	23	H2
Fieldings, The, Wok.	10	B2
Finch Rd, Guil.	7	F1
Finches Ri, Guil.	20	C6
Findlay Dr, Guil.	18	B4
Fir Gro, Wok.	10	C5
Fir Tree Rd, Wok.	19	F5
Firbank Dr, Wok.	10	D5
Firbank La, Wok.	10	D5
Fircroft Cl, Wok.	11	H4
Fircroft Ct, Wok.	11	H4
Fircroft Cl		
Firs, The, Guil.	22	D6
Firsway, Guil.	22	B1
Firwood Cl, Wok.	10	A5
Fitzjohn Cl, Guil.	20	C5
Fleetwood Ct, W.Byf.	9	G5
Florence Av, Add.	9	G3
Florida Rd, Guil.	27	G2
Flower Wk, Guil.	6	D6
Floyds La, Wok.	13	G2
Forbench Cl, Wok.	17	H2
Ford Rd (Old Woking), Wok.	12	B6
Forest Cl, Wok.	12	D1
Forest Rd, Wok.	12	D1
Foresters Cl, Wok.	10	B4
Forge End, Wok.	11	G3
Forsyth Path, Wok.	8	D5
Forsyth Rd, Wok.	8	C6
Forsythia Pl, Guil.	19	E6
Larch Av		
Fort Rd, Guil.	7	G6
Fosse Way, W.Byf.	9	F5
Brantwood Dr		
Four Acres, Guil.	20	C6
Fox Cl, Wok.	12	D1
Foxburrows Av, Guil.	22	B2
Foxenden Rd, Guil.	7	G2
Foxes Path, Guil.	15	H6
Foxglove Gdns, Guil.	20	C6
Foxglove Dr, Wok.	12	A1
Foxhanger Gdns, Wok.	12	A2
Oriental Rd		
Foxhills, Wok.	11	E3
Frailey Cl, Wok.	12	B2
Frailey Hill, Wok.	12	B2
Franklyn Ct, Guil.	22	B2
Humbolt Cl		
Franks Rd, Guil.	18	C6
French's Wells, Wok.	10	D3
Freshborough Ct, Guil.	23	H3
Lower Edgeborough Rd		
Friars Gate, Guil.	22	C4
Friars Ri, Wok.	12	A4
Friary Br, Guil.	6	D4
Friary Ct, Wok.	10	B4

Name	Page	Grid
Friary Pas, Guil.	6	D4
Friary St		
Friary Shop Cen, The, Guil.	6	D3
Onslow St		
Friary St, Guil.	6	D4
Frobisher Gdns, Guil.	24	A1
Frog La, Guil.	15	G5
Fulbrook Av, Add.	9	G3
Fullmer Way, Add.	9	F2
Furlough, The, Wok.	12	A3
Pembroke Rd		
Furze La, Gdmg.	26	B5
G		
Gables Cl, Wok.	11	H6
Kingfield Rd		
Gables Ct, Wok.	11	H6
Kingfield Rd		
Gales Cl, Guil.	20	D6
Gilliat Dr		
Galvins Cl, Guil.	18	C5
Ganghill, Guil.	20	A6
Gardner Rd, Guil.	23	E2
Gateway, The, Wok.	8	B6
Gateways, Guil.	24	A2
Gatley Dr, Guil.	19	H5
Genesis Business Pk, Wok.	12	C1
Genyn Rd, Guil.	6	B3
George Rd, Gdmg.	26	A6
George Rd, Guil.	7	E1
Georgelands (Ripley), Wok.	17	H1
Giffard Way, Guil.	18	C5
Gill Av, Guil.	22	A3
Gilliat Dr, Guil.	20	D6
Glade, The, W.Byf.	9	E5
Glebe Cotts, Guil.	21	H6
Glebe Ct, Guil.	23	H2
Glendale Cl, Wok.	11	E4
Glendale Dr, Guil.	20	B4
Gloster Rd, Wok.	12	A6
Gloucester Rd, Guil.	18	B6
Gloucester Sq, Wok.	11	G3
Church St E		
Gloucester Wk, Wok.	11	H3
Goldfinch Gdns, Guil.	24	D1
Goldfort Wk, Wok.	10	A2
Langmans Way		
Goldings, The, Wok.	10	B2
Goldsmiths Cl, Wok.	11	E4
Goldsworth Orchard, Wok.	10	C4
St. John's Rd		
Goldsworth Pk Trd Est, Wok.	10	D2
Goldsworth Rd, Wok.	11	E4
Golf Cl, Wok.	9	E6
Golf Club Rd, Wok.	10	C6
Goose La, Wok.	14	D2
Gorse Ct, Guil.	20	C6
Kingfisher Dr		
Gosden Cl, Guil.	27	G5
Gosden Common, Guil.	27	G5
Gosden Hill Rd, Guil.	20	C4
Gould Ct, Guil.	20	D6
Eustace Rd		
Grafton Cl, W.Byf.	9	F5
Madeira Rd		
Grandis Cotts, Guil.	17	H2
Grange Cl, Guil.	18	D4
Grange Pk, Wok.	11	G1
Grange Rd, Add.	9	G2
Grange Rd, Guil.	18	D3
Grangefields Rd, Guil.	19	F2
Grantley Cl, Guil.	27	G3
Grantley Gdns, Guil.	22	C1
Grantley Rd, Guil.	22	C1
Granville Rd, Wok.	11	H6
Grasmere Cl, Guil.	24	B1
Graylands, Wok.	11	G2
Graylands Cl, Wok.	11	G2
Grays Rd, Gdmg.	26	B6
Great Goodwin Dr, Guil.	20	B6
Great Oaks Pk, Guil.	20	B3
Great Quarry, Guil.	7	F6
Greatford Dr, Guil.	24	D2
Greatwood Cl, Cher.	8	C1
Green, The, Wok.	17	H1
Green Dr, Wok.	17	F3
Green La, Gdmg.	26	A4
Green La, Guil.	24	B2
Green La (West Clandon), Gui	21	G1
Green La (Mayford), Wok.	14	D1
Copper Beech Cl		
Greenacre, Wok.	10	A2
Mead Ct		
Greencroft, Guil.	24	B2
Greenham Wk, Wok.	11	E4
Greenheys Pl, Wok.	11	H4
White Rose La		
Greenhill Gdns, Guil.	20	C5

Name	Page	Grid
Greenmeads, Wok.	15	G2
Greenside Cl, Guil.	20	C6
Foxglove Gdns		
Greenway Cl, W.Byf.	9	G5
Greenways, Wok.	12	A3
Pembroke Rd		
Greenwood, The, Guil.	24	A2
Greenwood Cl, Add.	9	F3
Greenwood Rd, Wok.	10	A6
Gregory Cl, Wok.	11	E3
Greville Cl, Guil.	22	B2
Greyfriars Rd, Wok.	17	G4
Greythorne Rd, Wok.	10	C4
Grobars Av, Wok.	11	E1
Groom Wk, Guil.	19	G5
Grosvenor Ct, Guil.	20	A6
London Rd		
Grove, The, Guil.	11	H2
Grove Heath N, Wok.	17	H2
Grove Rd, Guil.	24	C2
Grove Rd, Wok.	11	H2
Guernsey Cl, Guil.	20	A3
Cotts Wd Dr		
Guernsey Fm Dr, Wok.	11	F1
Guildcroft, Guil.	24	A2
Guildford Business Pk, Guil.	22	D1
Guildford Bypass, Guil.	19	H5
Guildford La, Guil.	29	H1
Guildford La, Wok.	11	F6
Guildford Pk Av, Guil.	6	B2
Guildford Pk Rd, Guil.	6	B3
Guildford Rd, Gdmg.	26	C6
Guildford Rd, Guil.	19	F1
Guildford Rd, Wok.	11	G5
Guildford Rd (Mayford), Wok.	15	F2
Guildown Av, Guil.	22	D5
Guildown Rd, Guil.	22	D5
Guinness Ct, Wok.	10	B4
Iveagh Rd		
Gwynne Vaughan Av, Guil.	18	C4
H		
Hacketts La, Wok.	9	F6
Hale End, Wok.	14	D1
Halfpenny Cl, Guil.	28	D2
Halfpenny La, Guil.	24	C4
Hall Cl, Gdmg.	26	A6
Hall Dene Cl, Guil.	24	C1
Hall Pl, Wok.	12	A2
Halleys App, Wok.	10	C4
Halleys Ct, Wok.	10	C4
Halleys App		
Hallington Cl, Wok.	10	D3
Hamble Cl, Wok.	10	C3
Hamble Wk, Wok.	10	C4
Hamilton Av, Wok.	13	E1
Hamilton Cl, Guil.	18	C3
Hamilton Dr, Guil.	18	C3
Hamilton Gordon Ct, Guil.	23	E1
Langley Cl		
Hamilton Pl, Guil.	18	C3
Hammond Cl, Wok.	11	E1
Hammond Rd, Wok.	11	E1
Hanbury Path, Wok.	8	D6
Hanover Cl, Guil.	19	F6
Riverside		
Hanover Ct, Wok.	11	G5
Midhope Rd		
Hanson Cl, Guil.	19	H5
Hare Hill Cl, Wok.	13	G1
Harelands Cl, Wok.	11	E3
Harelands La, Wok.	11	E3
Hareward Rd, Guil.	20	C5
Harms Gro, Guil.	20	C5
Harrow La, Gdmg.	26	A6
Harts Gdns, Guil.	18	D5
Hartshill Wk, Wok.	10	D2
Harvey Rd, Guil.	7	G4
Hatfield Cl, W.Byf.	9	H4
Hawkswell Cl, Wok.	10	B3
Hawkswell Wk, Wok.	10	A3
Lockfield Dr		
Hawthorn Cl, Wok.	11	G6
Hawthorn Rd, Wok.	11	H6
Hawthorn Rd (Send Marsh), Wok.	17	G4
Hawthorne Way, Guil.	20	B6
Hayden Ct, Add.	9	H3
Haydon Pl, Guil.	7	E2
Hayes Barton, Wok.	12	D2
Haynes Cl, Wok.	17	H2
Hazel Av, Guil.	19	E4
Hazel Dr, Wok.	17	F5
Hazel Rd, W.Byf.	9	G6
Hazelhurst Cl, Guil.	20	B3
Weybrook Dr		
Hazelwood Rd, Wok.	10	A4
Heath Dr, Guil.	16	B2
Heath Ri, Wok.	17	H3
Heath Rd, Wok.	11	H1

Name	Page	Grid
Heathdown Rd, Wok.	12	D1
Heather Cl, Add.	9	H2
Heather Cl, Guil.	22	D1
Heather Cl, Wok.	11	E1
Heatherfields, Add.	9	H2
Heathervale Rd, Wok.	9	H2
Heathfield Cl, Wok.	12	A4
Heathfield Rd, Wok.	12	A4
Heathside Cres, Wok.	11	H3
Heathside Gdns, Wok.	12	A3
Heathside Pk Rd, Wok.	11	H4
Heathside Rd, Wok.	11	H4
Hedgerley Ct, Wok.	11	E3
Hedgeway, Guil.	22	C4
Helford Wk, Wok.	10	C4
Helmsdale, Wok.	10	D4
Winnington Way		
Henchley Dene, Guil.	20	D5
Henderson Av, Guil.	18	D3
Henley Bk, Guil.	22	C4
Henley Ct, Wok.	12	B6
Hennessy Ct, Wok.	8	C5
Henslow Way, Wok.	8	D6
Herbert Cres, Wok.	10	A3
Hereford Cl, Guil.	18	B6
Hereford Copse, Wok.	10	D5
Hermitage Rd, Wok.	10	B5
Hermitage Wds Cres, Wok.	10	A5
Heron Cl, Guil.	18	D5
Heron Wk, Wok.	8	C6
Blackmore Cres		
Heythorp Cl, Wok.	10	B3
Hidcote Cl, Wok.	12	B2
High Path Rd, Guil.	24	C2
High Pewley, Guil.	7	G5
High St, Guil.	7	E4
High St, Wok.	11	G3
High St (Horsell), Wok.	10	D1
High St (Old Woking), Wok.	16	B1
Highclere, Guil.	20	A6
Highcotts La, Guil.	17	F6
Highcotts La, Wok.	17	F5
Highfield, Guil.	27	G4
Highfield Cl, W.Byf.	9	G5
Highfield Rd, W.Byf.	9	G5
Highlands La, Wok.	15	G2
Highview, Wok.	10	A3
Mulgrave Way		
Hilgay, Guil.	23	H2
Hilgay Cl, Guil.	23	H2
Hill Cl, Wok.	11	F1
Hill Ct, Gdmg.	26	A6
Hill Vw Rd, Wok.	11	H4
Hillcrest Rd, Wok.	22	B1
Hillfield Cl, Guil.	20	C6
Hillier Rd, Guil.	24	A2
Hillmount, Wok.	11	G5
Constitution Hill		
Hillside, Wok.	11	F6
Hillspur Cl, Guil.	22	B1
Hillspur Rd, Guil.	22	B1
Hilltop Cl, Wok.	18	B4
Hillview Ct, Wok.	11	H4
Hillview Cres, Guil.	18	B6
Hipley Ct, Guil.	24	A3
Warren Rd		
Hipley St, Wok.	16	B3
Hitherbury Cl, Guil.	6	D6
Hobbs Cl, W.Byf.	9	H5
Hockering Gdns, Wok.	12	A3
Hockering Rd, Wok.	12	A4
Hodgson Gdns, Guil.	19	H5
Sutherland Dr		
Hoebrook Cl, Wok.	15	F1
Hogs Back, Guil.	22	A5
Holbreck Pl, Wok.	11	H4
Heathside Rd		
Holford Rd, Guil.	24	C2
Hollands, The, Wok.	11	G4
Montgomery Rd		
Hollies Av, W.Byf.	9	F5
Hollow Cl, Guil.	6	A3
Lynwood		
Holly Av, Add.	9	G2
Holly Bk Rd, Wok.	14	D1
Holly Cl, Wok.	10	D5
Holly Lea, Guil.	19	F2
Hollybank Rd, W.Byf.	9	G6
Holm Cl, Add.	9	E4
Holmes Cl, Wok.	15	H1
Holmesdale Cl, Guil.	24	B1
Holyoake Av, Wok.	11	E3
Holyoake Cres, Wok.	11	E3
Homefield Cl, Add.	9	E4
Honeypots Rd, Wok.	15	F2
Hook Heath Av, Wok.	10	D5
Hook Heath Gdns, Wok.	14	B1
Hook Heath Rd, Wok.	15	E1
Hook Hill La, Wok.	14	D1
Hook Hill Pk, Wok.	14	D1
Hopfield, Wok.	11	G2
Hopton Ct, Guil.	22	A2
Park Barn Dr		
Hornbeam Rd, Guil.	19	E5
Hornhatch, Guil.	28	B2
Hornhatch Cl, Guil.	28	B2
Hornhatch La, Guil.	28	A2
Horsell Birch, Wok.	10	D1
Horsell Moor, Wok.	11	F3
Horsell Pk, Wok.	11	F2
Horsell Pk Cl, Wok.	11	F2
Horsell Ri, Wok.	11	F1
Horsell Ri Cl, Wok.	11	F1
Horsell Vale, Wok.	11	G1
Horsell Way, Wok.	11	E2
Horseshoe La E, Guil.	24	B1
Horseshoe La W, Guil.	24	B1
Horsham Rd, Guil.	27	G4
Howard Gdns, Guil.	24	A1
Howard Ridge, Guil.	20	A4
Howards Cl, Wok.	12	A6
Howards Rd, Wok.	11	H6
Hudson Ct, Guil.	22	B1
Cobbett Rd		
Humbolt Cl, Guil.	22	A2
Hunter Rd, Guil.	7	H3
Huntingdon Rd, Wok.	10	B3
Hurley Gdns, Guil.	19	H4
Hurlford, Wok.	10	C3
Hurst Cl, Wok.	11	E6
Hurst Cft, Guil.	7	H6
Hurst Way, Wok.	9	E6
Huxley Rd, Guil.	22	A3

I

Name	Page	Grid
Inglehurst, Add.	9	H2
Inglewood, Wok.	10	D4
Inkerman Rd, Wok.	10	A4
Inkerman Way, Wok.	10	A4
Irwin Rd, Guil.	22	C3
Iveagh Rd, Guil.	6	A3
Iveagh Rd, Wok.	10	B4
Ivor Cl, Guil.	23	H3
Ivy La, Wok.	12	B4

J

Name	Page	Grid
Jackmans La, Wok.	10	C5
Jacob's Well Rd, Guil.	19	F3
James Rd, Guil.	27	E4
Janoway Hill La, Wok.	11	E5
Japonica Cl, Wok.	11	E4
Jasmine Cl, Wok.	10	B2
Jasons Dr, Guil.	20	C5
Jeffries Pas, Guil.	7	F3
High St		
Jenner Rd, Guil.	7	G3
Jersey Cl, Guil.	20	B3
Weybrook Dr		
John Russell Cl, Guil.	18	C5
Johnston Grn, Guil.	18	C4
Johnston Wk, Guil.	18	C4
Jordans Cl, Guil.	24	A1
Beatty Av		
Joseph's Rd, Guil.	23	E1
Julian Cl, Wok.	11	E4
Junewood Cl, Add.	9	F3
Juniper Cl, Guil.	18	D3
Juniper Pl, Guil.	27	F3
Juniper Ter, Guil.	27	F3

K

Name	Page	Grid
Kaye Ct, Guil.	19	E5
Keens La, Guil.	18	B4
Keens Pk Rd, Guil.	18	B4
Keepers Cl, Guil.	20	D5
Kemishford, Wok.	14	C3
Kent Rd, Wok.	12	B2
Kenton Way, Wok.	10	B3
Kerry Ter, Wok.	12	B2
Keston Av, Add.	9	G3
Kestrel Cl, Guil.	20	D6
Kevan Dr, Wok.	17	E4
Kiln La, Wok.	17	H4
Kilrush Ter, Wok.	12	A2
Kimber Ct, Guil.	20	D6
Gilliat Dr		
King Georges Dr, Add.	9	G2
Kingfield Cl, Wok.	11	H6
Kingfield Dr, Wok.	11	H6
Kingfield Gdns, Wok.	11	H6
Kingfield Grn, Wok.	11	H6
Kingfield Rd, Wok.	11	G6
Kingfisher Ct, Wok.	8	C6
Blackmore Cres		
Kingfisher Dr, Guil.	20	C6
Kinglake Ct, Wok.	10	A4
Raglan Rd		
Kings Rd, Add.	9	H2
Kings Rd, Guil.	23	F2
Kings Rd (Shalford), Guil.	27	G3
Kings Rd, Wok.	12	A2
Kingston Ri, Add.	9	G2
Kingsway, Wok.	11	F4
Kingsway Av, Wok.	11	F4
Kingswood Cl, Guil.	24	C1
Kirby Rd, Wok.	11	E3
Kirkefields, Guil.	18	C5
Kirkland Av, Wok.	10	A2
Knightswood, Wok.	10	B4
Knowl Hill, Wok.	12	B5
Knowle Gdns, W.Byf.	9	F5
Madeira Rd		
Knox Rd, Guil.	18	D4

L

Name	Page	Grid
Laburnum Cl, Guil.	19	E5
Laburnum Rd, Wok.	11	F6
Ladygrove Dr, Guil.	20	A3
Ladymead, Guil.	23	E1
Lakes Cl, Guil.	28	B2
Lakeside, Wok.	10	A5
Lakeside Cl, Wok.	10	A5
Laleham Ct, Wok.	11	G2
Lambourne Cres, Wok.	8	D5
Lampeter Cl, Wok.	11	G4
Lancaster Cl, Wok.	12	A2
Langdale Cl, Wok.	11	E2
Langley Cl, Guil.	23	E1
Langley Wk, Wok.	11	G5
Midhope Rd		
Langmans La, Wok.	10	D4
Langmans Way, Wok.	10	A2
Langshott Cl, Add.	9	E3
Langton Cl, Wok.	10	B3
Lansdown, Guil.	24	A2
Lansdown Cl, Wok.	10	B5
Lapwing Gro, Guil.	20	D6
Larch Av, Guil.	19	E6
Larches, The, Wok.	11	G2
Latimer Rd, Guil.	12	B2
Laundry Rd, Guil.	6	D2
Laurel Av, Wok.	8	D5
Laurel Cres, Wok.	8	C5
Laustan Cl, Guil.	24	C2
Lavender Pk Rd, W.Byf.	9	G4
Lavender Rd, Guil.	12	B2
Lawn Rd, Guil.	6	D6
Lawrence Cl, Guil.	20	B3
Ladygrove Dr		
Leafield Cl, Wok.	10	D4
Winnington Way		
Leapale La, Guil.	7	E3
Leapale Rd, Guil.	7	E3
Leas Rd, Guil.	6	D2
Ledger Cl, Guil.	20	B6
Leegate Cl, Wok.	10	D2
Sythwood		
Leisure La, W.Byf.	9	H4
Levylsdene, Guil.	24	D2
Liddington Hall Dr, Guil.	18	A5
Liddington New Rd, Guil.	18	A5
Lidstone Cl, Wok.	10	D3
Lilac Av, Wok.	11	F6
Lilac Cl, Guil.	19	E4
Lime Cl, Guil.	21	H2
Lime Gro, Guil.	18	D4
Lime Gro (West Clandon), Guil.	21	G2
Lime Gro, Wok.	15	G1
Limes, The, Wok.	11	F1
Lincoln Dr, Wok.	13	E1
Lincoln Rd, Guil.	18	B6
Linden Cl, Add.	9	G3
Linden Rd, Guil.	23	F2
Linden Way, Wok.	15	H1
Linden Way (Send Marsh), Wok.	17	F4
Lindfield Gdns, Guil.	23	H1
Lindsay Rd, Add.	9	G2
Lindvale, Wok.	11	G1
Link Av, Wok.	12	D1
Links Rd, Guil.	27	G6
Linkway, Guil.	22	B1
Linkway, Wok.	12	C3
Linnet Gro, Guil.	20	D6
Partridge Way		
Litchfield Way, Guil.	22	B4
Little Hide, Guil.	20	B6
Little Kiln, Gdmg.	26	A5
Little Mead, Wok.	10	B2
Little Moreton Cl, W.Byf.	9	H4
Little Orchard, Add.	9	F3
Little Orchard, Wok.	8	A6
Little Orchard Way, Guil.	27	G3
Little Riding, Wok.	12	B2
Little St, Guil.	18	D4
Little Warren Cl, Guil.	24	B4
Littleford La, Guil.	29	E4

Littleton La, Guil.	26	C1
Lock Cl, Add.	9	E5
Lock La, Wok.	13	H2
Lock Rd, Guil.	19	F5
Locke Way, Wok.	11	H3
The Bdy		
Lockfield Dr, Wok.	10	B4
Lockner Holt, Guil.	29	F3
Locksley Dr, Wok.	10	B4
Robin Hood Rd		
Lockwood Path, Guil.	8	D5
Loder Cl, Wok.	8	D5
Lombardy Cl, Wok.	10	B3
Nethercote Av		
London Rd, Guil.	7	H2
London Rd, Wok.	20	C2
London Sq, Guil.	7	H1
Long Dyke, Guil.	20	B6
Long Gore, Gdmg.	26	A4
Longbourne Grn, Gdmg.	26	A5
Barnes Rd		
Longdown Rd, Guil.	24	B5
Longmead, Guil.	24	C2
Longridge Gro, Wok.	9	E6
Old Woking Rd		
Longs Cl, Wok.	13	G2
Loop Rd, Wok.	15	H1
Loseley Pk, Guil.	26	B2
Loseley Rd, Gdmg.	26	A5
Lovelace Dr, Wok.	13	F1
Lower Edgeborough Rd, Guil.	23	H3
Lower Sandfields, Wok.	16	D4
Lowthorpe, Wok.	10	C4
Shilburn Way		
Lucerne Cl, Wok.	11	G5
Claremont Av		
Ludlow Rd, Guil.	6	B3
Lych Way, Wok.	11	F2
Lydele Cl, Wok.	11	H1
Lyndale Ct, W.Byf.	9	G5
Parvis Rd		
Lyndhurst Cl, Wok.	11	F1
Lynwood, Guil.	6	A2
Lynwood Cl, Wok.	8	D5
Lyons Dr, Guil.	18	C3
Lytton Rd, Wok.	12	B2

M

Mabel St, Wok.	11	F3
Madeira Cl, W.Byf.	9	G5
Brantwood Gdns		
Madeira Cres, W.Byf.	9	G5
Brantwood Gdns		
Madeira Rd, W.Byf.	9	F5
Madrid Rd, Guil.	6	A3
Maitland Cl, W.Byf.	9	G5
Malacca Fm, Guil.	21	H1
Mallow Cres, Guil.	20	B5
Mandeville Cl, Guil.	18	C5
Mangles Rd, Guil.	19	F6
Manor Cl, Wok.	13	F2
Manor Cres, Guil.	18	D6
Manor Dr, Add.	9	G2
Manor Gdns, Gdmg.	26	A6
Farncombe St		
Manor Gdns, Guil.	18	D6
Manor Lo, Guil.	18	D6
Manor Rd, Guil.	18	D6
Manor Rd, Guil.	11	E2
Manor Rd (Send Marsh), Wok.	17	F3
Manor Way, Guil.	22	A5
Manor Way, Wok.	16	B1
Mansel Cl, Guil.	18	D3
Manston Rd, Guil.	20	A4
Maori Rd, Guil.	23	H2
Maple Gro, Guil.	19	F6
Maple Gro, Wok.	15	G1
Maple Rd, Wok.	17	G4
Mareschal Rd, Guil.	6	C5
Margaret Rd, Guil.	6	D2
Marjoram Cl, Guil.	18	C4
Markenfield Rd, Guil.	7	E1
Market Sq, Wok.	11	G3
Cawsey Way		
Market St, Guil.	7	E3
Marlborough Rd, Wok.	12	A2
Marlyns Cl, Guil.	20	A4
Marlyns Dr, Guil.	20	A4
Marston Rd, Wok.	10	D3
Martin Rd, Guil.	18	C6
Martin Way, Wok.	10	C4
Martindale Cl, Guil.	20	D6
Gilliat Dr		
Martindale Rd, Wok.	10	B4
Martins Cl, Guil.	24	C1
Martinsyde, Wok.	12	C3
Martyr Rd, Guil.	7	E3
Martyrs La, Wok.	8	B4
Mary Rd, Guil.	6	D2

Mathon Ct, Guil.	23	H2
Cross Las		
Maybourne Ri, Wok.	15	F4
Maybury Hill, Wok.	12	B2
Maybury Rd, Wok.	11	H3
Mayfield Av, Add.	9	H2
Mayford Cl, Wok.	15	F2
Mayford Grn, Wok.	15	F2
Smarts Heath Rd		
Mayhurst Av, Wok.	12	C2
Mayhurst Cl, Wok.	12	C2
Mayhurst Cres, Wok.	12	C2
Mays Gro, Wok.	16	D3
Maysfield Rd, Wok.	16	D3
Maytree Cl, Guil.	18	D5
Mead Ct, Wok.	10	A2
Mead Way, Guil.	20	C3
Meadow Bungalows, Guil.	28	B2
Meadow Cl, Gdmg.	26	A6
Meadow Dr, Wok.	17	F3
Meadow Rd, Guil.	20	A4
Meadowlands, Guil.	21	H4
Meadows, The, Guil.	23	E5
Meads Rd, Guil.	24	A2
Meadway Dr, Wok.	11	E2
Medlar Cl, Guil.	19	E6
Melbury Cl, W.Byf.	9	G6
Mellersh Hill Rd, Guil.	28	B6
Mercia Wk, Wok.	11	H3
Church St W		
Merlin Ct, Wok.	8	C6
Blackmore Cres		
Merrivale Gdns, Wok.	11	E3
Merrow Business Cen, Guil.	20	C5
Merrow La		
Merrow Chase, Guil.	24	C2
Merrow Common Rd, Guil.	20	C5
Merrow Copse, Guil.	24	B1
Merrow Ct, Guil.	24	D2
Levylsdene		
Merrow Cft, Guil.	24	C1
Merrow Downs, Guil.	24	D3
Merrow La, Guil.	20	C3
Merrow St, Guil.	20	D6
Merrow Way, Guil.	24	D1
Merrow Wds, Guil.	20	B6
Mews, The, Guil.	6	C2
Walnut Tree Cl		
Meyrick Cl, Wok.	10	A2
Middle Wk, Wok.	11	G3
Commercial Way		
Midhope Cl, Wok.	11	G5
Midhope Gdns, Wok.	11	G5
Midhope Rd		
Midhope Rd, Wok.	11	G5
Midleton Ind Est, Guil.	22	D1
Midleton Ind Est Rd, Guil.	22	D1
Midleton Rd, Guil.	22	D1
Milcombe Cl, Wok.	10	D4
Inglewood		
Mile Path, Wok.	10	D6
Milestone Cl, Wok.	17	G2
Milkhouse Gate, Guil.	7	F4
High St		
Mill La, Guil.	7	E4
Quarry Rd		
Mill La (Chilworth), Guil.	29	F1
Mill La (Peasmarsh), Guil.	26	D4
Millan Cl, Add.	9	H2
Millbrook, Guil.	7	E4
Miller Rd, Guil.	20	C5
Millford, Wok.	10	D3
Millmead, Guil.	6	D4
Millmead Ter, Guil.	6	D5
Mint Wk, Wok.	10	A3
Mitchells Cl, Guil.	27	G2
Station Rd		
Mitchells Row, Guil.	27	G3
Molloy Ct, Wok.	12	A2
Courtenay Rd		
Molyneux Rd, Gdmg.	26	B6
Monro Dr, Guil.	18	C5
Montgomerie Dr, Guil.	18	C3
Montgomery Rd, Wok.	11	G4
Monument Rd, Wok.	8	A6
Monument Way E, Wok.	12	B1
Monument Way W, Wok.	12	A1
Moor La, Wok.	15	G2
Moorfield Rd, Guil.	19	F4
Moorholme, Wok.	11	G5
Oakbank		
Moorlands, The, Wok.	15	H1
Morcote Cl, Guil.	27	G3
More Circle, Gdmg.	26	A6
More Rd, Gdmg.	26	A6
Morton Cl, Wok.	11	E1
Morton Rd, Wok.	11	E1
Mount, The, Guil.	6	B6
Mount, The, Wok.	11	F4

Mount, The (Saint John's), Wok.	10	C5
Mount Cl, Wok.	14	D1
Mount Hermon Cl, Wok.	11	F4
Mount Hermon Rd, Wok.	11	F5
Mount Pl, Guil.	6	D4
The Mt		
Mount Pleasant, Guil.	6	D4
Mount Rd, Wok.	14	D1
Mountside, Guil.	6	B5
Moyne Ct, Wok.	11	F4
Iveagh Rd		
Muirfield Rd, Wok.	10	C4
Mulberry Ct, Guil.	20	D5
Gilliat Dr		
Mulgrave Way, Wok.	10	A4
Munstead Vw, Guil.	22	D6
Murray Grn, Wok.	8	C6
Bunyard Dr		

N

Napier Gdns, Guil.	24	B1
Nelson Gdns, Guil.	24	A1
Nether Mt, Guil.	6	B5
Nethercote Av, Wok.	10	B3
Nettles Ter, Guil.	7	E1
New Coppice, Wok.	10	A5
New Cross Rd, Guil.	18	C6
New Inn La, Guil.	20	B4
New La, Guil.	15	G2
New Rd (Chilworth), Guil.	28	B3
New Rd (Wonersh), Guil.	28	B5
Newark Cl, Guil.	20	B3
Dairyman's Wk		
Newark Cl, Wok.	17	G1
Newark Cotts, Wok.	17	G1
Newark La, Wok.	13	F4
Newlands Av, Wok.	15	H1
Newlands Cor, Guil.	25	G4
Newsham Rd, Guil.	10	B3
Nicholas Gdns, Wok.	13	E2
Nightingale Rd, Guil.	23	F2
Norfolk Fm Cl, Wok.	12	D2
Norfolk Fm Rd, Wok.	12	D1
North Downs Way, Guil.	22	B6
North Moors, Guil.	19	G4
North Pl, Guil.	7	E2
North Rd, Guil.	18	D5
North Rd, Wok.	12	A2
North St, Gdmg.	26	B6
Station Rd		
North St, Guil.	7	E3
Northbourne, Gdmg.	26	B5
Northdown La, Guil.	7	H6
Northfield, Guil.	27	G4
Northway, Guil.	18	C6
Nottingham Rd, Wok.	10	B4
Nottingham Ct, Wok.	10	B4
Nottingham Cl		
Nursery Cl, Add.	9	F2
Nursery Cl, Wok.	11	E2
Nursery Gdns, Guil.	28	B2
Nursery Rd, Gdmg.	26	B6

O

Oak Cl, Gdmg.	26	A5
Oak End Way, Add.	9	E4
Oak Gra Rd, Guil.	21	H2
Oak Hill, Guil.	20	C3
Oak La, Wok.	12	C2
Beaufort Rd		
Oak Pk, W.Byf.	9	E5
Oak Tree Cl (Burpham), Guil.	20	B3
Oak Tree Cl (Jacobs Well), Guil.	19	E2
Oak Tree Dr, Guil.	19	E4
Oakbank, Wok.	11	G5
Oakcroft Cl, W.Byf.	9	F6
Oakcroft Rd, W.Byf.	9	F6
Oakdene Rd, Wok.	27	E4
Oakfield, Wok.	10	A2
Oakfields, Guil.	18	B6
Oakfields, W.Byf.	9	H6
Oaklands Cl, Guil.	27	G4
Oakley Dell, Guil.	20	C5
Oaks, The, W.Byf.	9	G5
Oaks Rd, Wok.	11	G3
Oakway, Wok.	10	A5
Oakwood, Guil.	18	C3
Oakwood Rd, Wok.	10	A5
Ockenden Cl, Wok.	11	H4
Ockenden Rd		
Ockenden Gdns, Wok.	11	H4
Ockenden Rd		
Ockenden Rd, Wok.	11	H4
Ockley Ct, Guil.	20	B3
Cotts Wd Dr		
Old Acre, Wok.	9	G6
Old Av, W.Byf.	9	E5
Old Av Cl, W.Byf.	9	E5
Old Bakery Ms, Guil.	29	H1

Name	Page	Grid
Old Ct Rd, Guil.	22	C3
Old Fm Rd, Guil.	19	F5
Old Hill, Wok.	11	F6
Old Malt Way, Wok.	11	F3
Old Manor Gdns, Guil.	28	D2
Old Manor La, Guil.	28	C2
Old Merrow St, Guil.	20	C5
Old Palace Rd, Guil.	22	C3
Old Portsmouth Rd, Gdmg.	26	D4
Old Portsmouth Rd, Guil.	26	D4
Old Sch Pl, Wok.	15	G1
Old Woking Rd, W.Byf.	9	F5
Old Woking Rd, Wok.	13	E2
Oldfield Wd, Wok.	12	B3
Maybury Hill		
Omega Rd, Wok.	12	A1
One Tree Hill Rd, Guil.	24	B3
Onslow Cl, Wok.	12	A3
Onslow Cres, Wok.	12	A3
Onslow Rd, Guil.	7	F1
Onslow St, Guil.	6	D3
Onslow Vw, Guil.	13	F1
Orchard, The, Wok.	15	G2
Orchard Av, Add.	9	F3
Orchard Cl, Guil.	24	B2
Orchard Cl, Guil.	12	B2
Orchard Dr, Wok.	11	H1
Orchard Fld Rd, Gdmg.	26	B6
Orchard Lea Cl, Wok.	13	E1
Orchard Mains, Wok.	11	E5
Orchard Rd, Guil.	22	B4
Orchard Rd (Burpham), Guil.	20	B4
Orchard Rd (Shalford), Guil.	27	G2
Orchard Way, Wok.	16	C5
Orchards Cl, W.Byf.	9	G6
Oregano Way, Guil.	18	C3
Oriental Cl, Wok.	12	A3
Oriental Rd		
Oriental Rd, Wok.	12	A3
Ormonde Rd, Wok.	11	E2
Oval, The, Gdmg.	26	B6
Oval, The, Guil.	22	C3
Overthorpe Cl, Wok.	10	A3
Ovington Ct, Wok.	10	B2
Roundthorn Way		
Oxford Rd, Guil.	7	F4
Oxford Ter, Guil.	7	F4
Pewley Hill		
P		
Paddock, The, Guil.	24	D1
Paddock Way, Wok.	8	B6
Paddocks, The, Add.	9	H2
Paddocks Mead, Wok.	10	A2
Paddocks Rd, Guil.	20	A4
Palm Gro, Guil.	19	E3
Palmer's Lo, Guil.	22	C3
Old Palace Rd		
Pannells Ct, Guil.	7	F3
Pantiles Cl, Wok.	10	D4
Papercourt La, Wok.	17	F2
Pares Cl, Wok.	11	F2
Park Barn Dr, Guil.	18	A6
Park Barn E, Guil.	22	B1
Park Chase, Guil.	7	G1
Park Cl, Add.	9	H2
Park Cl, W.Byf.	9	G5
Park Ct, Wok.	11	H4
Park Dr		
Park Dr, Wok.	11	H4
Park La, Guil.	20	C5
Park Pl, Wok.	11	H4
Park Dr		
Park Rd, Guil.	7	E1
Park Rd, Wok.	12	A3
Park St, Guil.	6	D4
Park Vw Ct, Wok.	11	G5
Parkhurst Rd, Wok.	22	C1
Parklands Pl, Guil.	24	B2
Parkside, Add.	9	H2
Parkview Vale, Guil.	20	C6
Foxglove Gdns		
Parkway, Guil.	23	G1
Parley Dr, Wok.	11	E3
Parsons Grn, Guil.	19	F6
Bellfields Rd		
Parsons Grn Ct, Guil.	19	F6
Bellfields Rd		
Partridge Way, Guil.	20	D6
Parvis Rd, W.Byf.	9	H5
Pathway, The, Wok.	17	F5
Paxton Gdns, Wok.	9	E4
Peacocks Cen, The, Wok.	11	G3
Peak Rd, Guil.	18	C5
Pearl Ct, Wok.	10	A2
Langmans Way		
Peatmore Av, Wok.	13	G2
Peatmore Cl, Wok.	13	G2
Pembroke Gdns, Wok.	12	A4
Pembroke Rd, Wok.	12	A4
Pendennis Cl, W.Byf.	9	G6
Pennings Av, Guil.	18	B6
Pentreath Av, Guil.	22	B3
Penwith Wk, Wok.	11	F5
Wych Hill Pk		
Penwood End, Wok.	14	D1
Percy Rd, Guil.	18	D6
Perleybrooke La, Wok.	10	C3
Bampton Way		
Perrin Ct, Wok.	12	B1
Blackmore Cres		
Perrior Rd, Gdmg.	26	A6
Perry Hill, Guil.	18	A2
Peterborough Rd, Guil.	18	B6
Pewley Bk, Guil.	7	H4
Pewley Hill, Guil.	7	F4
Pewley Pt, Guil.	7	H5
Pewley Way, Guil.	7	H4
Phillips Hatch, Guil.	28	C5
Phoenix Ct, Guil.	6	D3
High St		
Piccards, The, Guil.	23	E6
Chestnut Av		
Pilgrims Way, Guil.	23	F6
Pimms Cl, Guil.	20	A4
Pine Cl, Add.	9	H3
Pine Cl, Wok.	11	E3
Pine Rd, Wok.	11	E6
Pine Tree Hill, Wok.	12	D2
Pine Vw Cl, Guil.	29	F2
Pinewood Cl, Wok.	8	A6
Pinewood Gro, Add.	9	H2
Pinewood Pk, Add.	9	H3
Pit Fm Rd, Guil.	24	A2
Platt Meadow, Guil.	20	D5
Eustace Rd		
Polesden La, Wok.	17	F2
Pollard Rd, Wok.	12	B2
Poltimore Rd, Guil.	22	C4
Pond Meadow, Guil.	22	A2
Pond Rd, Wok.	10	C6
Pondfield Rd, Gdmg.	26	B6
Poole Rd, Wok.	11	G3
Poplar Gro, Wok.	11	G5
Poplar Rd, Guil.	27	G3
Porridge Pot All, Guil.	6	D5
Bury Flds		
Portsmouth Rd, Guil.	23	E6
Portugal Rd, Wok.	12	A2
Potters La, Wok.	16	B3
Pound Fld, Guil.	23	F1
Pound Pl, Guil.	27	H2
Pound Pl Cl, Guil.	27	H2
Poundfield Ct, Wok.	16	C1
High St		
Poundfield Gdns, Wok.	12	C6
Powell Cl, Guil.	22	B4
Poyle Rd, Guil.	7	G5
Poyle Ter, Guil.	7	F4
Sydenham Rd		
Prae, The, Wok.	13	F4
Prestbury Ct, Wok.	10	C4
Muirfield Rd		
Prey Heath, Wok.	14	D3
Prey Heath Cl, Wok.	15	E4
Prey Heath Rd, Wok.	14	D4
Priestly Gdns, Wok.	12	A6
Princess Gdns, Wok.	12	B2
Princess Rd, Wok.	12	B2
Priors Ct, Wok.	10	C4
Priors Cft, Wok.	12	A6
Priory Cl, Wok.	8	D5
Priory Ct, Guil.	23	E5
Portsmouth Rd		
Providence Pl, Wok.	9	G6
Purbeck Ct, Guil.	22	A2
Egerton Rd		
Pyle Hill, Wok.	15	F4
Pyrford Common Rd, Wok.	12	D2
Pyrford Ct, Wok.	13	E3
Pyrford Heath, Wok.	13	F2
Pyrford Rd, W.Byf.	9	G5
Pyrford Rd, Wok.	9	G6
Pyrford Wds Cl, Wok.	13	F1
Pyrford Wds Rd, Wok.	13	E1
Q		
Quadrangle, The, Guil.	22	C3
The Oval		
Quarry St, Guil.	7	E4
Quartermaine Av, Wok.	15	H2
Queen Eleanor's Rd, Guil.	22	B3
Queen Elizabeth Way, Wok.	11	H5
Queen Mary Cl, Wok.	12	C2
Queen Marys Dr, Add.	9	F2
Queendale Ct, Wok.	10	B2
Roundthorn Way		
Queenhythe Rd, Guil.	19	F2
Queens Ct, Wok.	11	H4
Hill Vw Rd		
Queens Dr, Guil.	18	C5
Queens Rd, Guil.	7	F1
Quintrell Cl, Wok.	10	D3
R		
Racks Ct, Guil.	7	F5
Radstone Ct, Wok.	11	H4
Raeburn Ct, Wok.	10	C4
Martin Way		
Raglan Rd, Wok.	10	A4
Rainbow Ct, Wok.	10	A2
Langmans Way		
Ramin Ct, Guil.	19	E5
Rowan Cl		
Randolph Cl, Wok.	10	A3
Creston Av		
Ravenswood Ct, Wok.	11	H4
Raymond Cres, Guil.	22	B3
Recreation Rd, Guil.	23	E2
Rectory Cl, Guil.	20	D6
Redcourt, Wok.	12	D1
Redwing Gdns, W.Byf.	9	H4
Redwing Ri, Guil.	20	D6
Redwood Gro, Guil.	28	C2
Reed Pl, W.Byf.	9	E5
Regalfield Cl, Guil.	18	C4
Regan Cl, Guil.	18	D3
Regency Dr, W.Byf.	9	F5
Regency Way, Wok.	12	D1
Reindorp Cl, Guil.	22	C3
Old Ct Rd		
Rices Cor, Guil.	28	A3
Ridge, The, Wok.	12	B3
Ridge Cl, Wok.	14	D1
Ridgemount, Guil.	6	A2
Ridges, The, Guil.	27	E1
Ridgeway, Wok.	11	F1
Ridgeway, The, Guil.	24	A3
Ridgeway Cl, Wok.	11	F2
Ridgeway Gdns, Wok.	11	F1
Ridgway, Wok.	13	G1
Ridgway Rd, Wok.	13	F1
Riding, The, Wok.	8	B6
Ridings, The, Wok.	17	G3
Ridsdale Rd, Wok.	10	D3
Ringmore Dr, Guil.	20	C5
Ripon Cl, Guil.	18	B6
River Wey Navigation, Guil.	20	B6
River Wey Navigation, Wok.	16	B2
Riverdale Dr, Wok.	15	H1
Rivermount Gdns, Guil.	23	E5
Riverside, Guil.	19	F6
Riverside Dr, Guil.	28	A6
Riverside Gdns, Wok.	16	B1
Riverway Est, Guil.	27	E4
Rivett Drake Rd, Guil.	18	C4
Rivey Cl, W.Byf.	9	F6
Robertson Ct, Wok.	10	A4
Raglan Rd		
Robin Hood Cl, Wok.	10	B4
Robin Hood Cres, Wok.	10	A3
Robin Hood La, Wok.	15	H4
Robin Hood Rd, Wok.	10	B4
Robin Way, Guil.	18	D4
Rodney Way, Guil.	24	A1
Roffords, Wok.	10	C4
Rokeby Cl, Wok.	10	B3
Romans Way, Wok.	13	G1
Rookwood Ct, Guil.	6	C6
Rose Bk Cotts, Wok.	15	G2
Roseacre Gdns, Guil.	29	F2
Rosebery Cres, Wok.	15	H1
Rosebriar Cl, Wok.	13	G2
Rosehill Av, Wok.	11	E2
Rosemary Cres, Guil.	18	B4
Rosemount Av, W.Byf.	9	G5
Rosetrees, Guil.	24	A3
Rosewarne Cl, Wok.	10	C4
Muirfield Rd		
Rosewood, Wok.	12	A5
Roslyn Ct, Wok.	10	C4
St. John's Rd		
Roughlands, Wok.	13	E1
Roundhill, Wok.	12	B5
Roundhill Dr, Wok.	12	B4
Roundhill Way, Wok.	22	B2
Roundthorn Way, Wok.	10	B2
Rowan Cl, Guil.	18	D5
Rowans, The, Wok.	11	G4
Rowbury, Gdmg.	26	C5
Rowley Cl, Wok.	13	G2
Royal Oak Rd, Wok.	11	E4
Runtley Wd La, Guil.	15	H5
Rupert Rd, Guil.	6	B3
Ruscoe Dr, Wok.	12	A3
Pembroke Rd		
Rush Cft, Gdmg.	26	C5

Name	Page	Grid
Rushmoor Cl, Guil.	18	B5
Russell Cl, Wok.	11	E1
Russell Ct, Guil.	19	E5
Rowan Cl		
Russell Rd, Wok.	11	E1
Russetts Cl, Wok.	11	H1
Ryde Heron, Wok.	10	A3
Robin Hood Rd		
Rydens Way, Wok.	12	A6
Rydes Av, Guil.	18	B5
Rydes Cl, Wok.	12	C6
Rydes Hill Cres, Guil.	18	B4
Rydes Hill Rd, Guil.	18	B6
Rye Cl, Guil.	18	A6
S		
Sadlers Cl, Guil.	24	D1
Saffron Platt, Guil.	18	C4
St. Andrews Cl, Wok.	11	E3
St. Mary's Rd		
St. Bartholomews Ct, Guil.	23	H3
St. Catherines, Wok.	11	E5
St. Catherines Dr, Guil.	22	D6
St. Catherines Hill, Guil.	23	E6
Portsmouth Rd		
St. Catherines Pk, Guil.	23	H4
St. Crispins Way, Cher.	8	C1
St. James Cl, Wok.	10	C4
St. John's Cl, Guil.	22	C3
St. John's Rd		
St. John's Ct, Wok.	10	C5
St. Johns Hill Rd		
St. Johns Hill Rd, Wok.	10	C5
St. John's Lye, Wok.	10	B5
St. Johns Ms, Wok.	10	C5
St. Johns Ri, Wok.	10	D5
St. John's Rd, Guil.	22	B3
St. John's Rd, Wok.	10	D4
St. John's St, Gdmg.	26	B6
St. Lukes Sq, Guil.	23	H3
St. Margarets, Guil.	23	H1
St. Martha's Av, Wok.	15	H1
St. Martins Ms, Wok.	13	G2
St. Mary's Rd, Wok.	11	E3
St. Mary's Way, Guil.	18	A6
St. Michael's Rd, Wok.	8	D6
St. Mildreds Rd, Guil.	23	H1
St. Nicholas Cres, Wok.	13	G2
St. Omer Ridge, Guil.	24	A3
St. Omer Rd, Guil.	24	A3
St. Pauls Rd, Wok.	12	A3
St. Peters Cl, Wok.	12	C6
St. Peters Rd, Wok.	16	B1
St. Saviours Pl, Guil.	6	D1
Leas Rd		
St. Thomas Cl, Wok.	11	E3
St. Mary's Rd		
St. Thomas's Ms, Guil.	23	H4
St. Catherines Pk		
Salisbury Rd, Wok.	11	G5
Salt Box Rd, Guil.	18	B3
Sample Oak La, Guil.	29	E2
Sandalwood, Guil.	6	A3
Sandfield Ter, Guil.	7	F2
Sandfields, Wok.	16	D4
Sandringham Cl, Wok.	13	G2
Sandy Cl, Wok.	12	B3
Sandy La		
Sandy La, Guil.	26	C1
Sandy La, Wok.	12	C2
Sandy La (Pyrford), Wok.	13	F3
Sandy La (Send), Wok.	16	C3
Sandy Way, Wok.	12	C3
Sanger Dr, Wok.	16	C3
Sappho Ct, Wok.	10	A2
Langmans Way		
Saunders Copse, Wok.	14	D2
Saunders La, Wok.	14	A2
Scarlett Cl, Wok.	10	B4
Bingham Dr		
Scholars Wk, Guil.	6	B2
School Cl, Guil.	19	F6
Scillonian Rd, Guil.	22	C3
Scotland Br Rd, Add.	9	G3
Scott Cl, Guil.	18	C6
Scylla Pl, Wok.	10	C5
Church Rd		
Selbourne Av, Add.	9	H2
Selbourne Cl, Add.	9	H1
Selbourne Rd, Add.	20	A5
Selby Wk, Wok.	10	D4
Wyndham Rd		
Selhurst Cl, Wok.	11	H1
Selsdon Rd, Add.	9	G3
Selwood Rd, Wok.	12	B6
Semaphore Rd, Guil.	7	G5
Semper Cl, Wok.	10	A3
Send Barns La, Wok.	16	D4
Send Cl, Wok.	16	C3
Send Hill, Wok.	16	C5
Send Marsh Rd, Wok.	17	F3
Send Par Cl, Wok.	16	C3
Send Rd		
Send Rd, Wok.	16	B2
Shackleford Rd, Wok.	12	A6
Shackleton Wk, Guil.	22	B2
Humbolt Cl		
Shaftesbury Rd, Wok.	12	A3
Shalford Rd, Guil.	7	F6
Sheep Wk, The, Wok.	13	E4
Sheepfold Rd, Guil.	18	B5
Sheeplands Av, Guil.	20	C6
Sheerwater Rd, Add.	9	E4
Sheerwater Business Cen, Wok.	8	C6
Sheerwater Rd, Add.	9	E4
Sheerwater Rd, W.Byf.	9	E4
Sheldon Ct, Guil.	23	H3
Lower Edgeborough Rd		
Shelton Cl, Guil.	18	C3
Shepherds Hill, Guil.	18	C6
Shepherds La, Guil.	18	B5
Shepherds Way, Guil.	23	G6
Sherwood Rd, Wok.	10	A3
Shetland Cl, Guil.	20	B3
Weybrook Dr		
Shey Copse, Wok.	12	C3
Shilburn Way, Wok.	10	C4
Shimmings, The, Guil.	24	A1
Silo Cl, Gdmg.	26	B5
Silo Dr, Gdmg.	26	B5
Silo Rd, Gdmg.	26	B5
Silver Birch Cl, Add.	9	E4
Silversmiths Way, Wok.	11	E4
Slapleys, Wok.	11	F6
Slocock Hill, Wok.	11	E3
Slyfield Ct, Guil.	19	G4
Slyfield Grn		
Slyfield Grn, Guil.	19	F4
Slyfield Ind Est, Guil.	19	G4
Smarts Heath La, Wok.	14	C3
Smarts Heath Rd, Wok.	14	B3
Somerswey, Guil.	27	G4
Somertons Cl, Guil.	18	C5
South Cl, Wok.	11	E2
South Hill, Guil.	7	F4
South Rd, Guil.	18	D6
South Vw Ct, Wok.	11	G4
Constitution Hill		
Southcote, Wok.	11	F1
Southway, Guil.	22	B2
Southway Ct, Guil.	22	A2
Soyer Ct, Wok.	10	A4
Raglan Rd		
Speedwell Cl, Guil.	20	B5
Spencer Cl, Wok.	8	C5
Spring Cl, Gdmg.	26	A5
Spring Ct, Guil.	18	D4
Dayspring		
Spring Gro, Gdmg.	26	A5
Springfield Cl, Wok.	10	A4
Springfield Rd, Guil.	7	G2
Springhaven Cl, Guil.	24	A2
Springside Ct, Guil.	23	E1
Square, The, Guil.	22	B4
Orchard Rd		
Squirrel Keep, W.Byf.	9	H4
Squirrel Wd, W.Byf.	9	H4
Stables, The, Guil.	19	F5
Old Fm Rd		
Stag Hill, Guil.	22	C3
Stainton Wk, Wok.	11	E4
Inglewood		
Stakescorner Rd, Guil.	26	C4
Stanley Rd, Wok.	11	H2
Stantons Wf, Guil.	28	A4
Star Hill, Guil.	11	E5
Station App, Guil.	7	G2
Station App, W.Byf.	9	G4
Station App, Wok.	11	H3
Station Pl, Gdmg.	26	B6
Summers Rd		
Station Rd, Gdmg.	26	B6
Station Rd, Guil.	27	G2
Station Rd, W.Byf.	9	G4
Station Row, Guil.	27	G2
Station Vw, Guil.	6	C2
Staveley Way, Wok.	10	A3
Stepbridge Path, Wok.	11	F3
Goldsworth Rd		
Stewart Cl, Wok.	10	B3
Nethercote Av		
Stockers La, Wok.	11	H6
Stocton Cl, Guil.	23	E1
Stocton Rd, Guil.	23	E1
Stoke Flds, Guil.	7	F2
York Rd		
Stoke Gro, Guil.	7	F1
Stoke Rd		
Stoke Ms, Guil.	7	F2
Stoke Rd		
Stoke Rd, Guil.	23	F1
Stonebridge Flds, Guil.	27	F3
Stonebridge Wf, Guil.	27	F3
Stonecrop Rd, Guil.	20	C6
Kingfisher Dr		
Stoney Brook, Guil.	22	A1
Stoop Ct, W.Byf.	9	H4
Stoughton Rd, Guil.	18	C5
Street, The (Albury), Guil.	29	H1
Street, The (Shalford), Guil.	27	G1
Street, The (West Clandon), Guil.	21	H5
Street, The (Wonersh), Guil.	28	A6
Stringers Av, Guil.	19	F2
Stringer's Common, Guil.	19	E3
Stringhams Copse, Wok.	17	F4
Struan Gdns, Wok.	11	G1
Sturt Ct, Guil.	20	B6
Suffolk Dr, Guil.	20	B3
Summers Rd, Gdmg.	26	B6
Summersbury Dr, Guil.	27	G4
Sun Hill, Guil.	14	C1
Sundridge Rd, Wok.	12	A5
Sutherland Av, Guil.	19	F2
Sutherland Dr, Guil.	19	H5
Sutton Av, Guil.	10	A5
Sutton Grn Rd, Guil.	15	G6
Sutton Pk, Guil.	19	H1
Swan Ct, Guil.	19	F6
Swan La, Guil.	7	E3
Swaynes La, Guil.	25	E2
Sycamore Rd, Guil.	23	F2
Sydenham Rd, Guil.	7	F4
Sydney Pl, Guil.	23	H3
Sydney Rd, Guil.	23	H3
Sylvan Cl, Wok.	12	B3
Sythwood, Wok.	10	D3
T		
Tamarind Cl, Guil.	18	C3
Tamerton Sq, Wok.	11	G5
Tangier Rd, Guil.	24	A3
Tanglewood Cl, Wok.	12	D2
Tangley La, Guil.	18	B4
Tannersfield, Guil.	27	G4
Tannery La, Guil.	27	G6
Tannery La, Wok.	17	F2
Tansy Cl, Guil.	20	C6
Tarragon Dr, Guil.	18	C3
Teggs La, Wok.	13	F2
Telford Ct, Guil.	23	G3
Clandon Rd		
Temple Bar Rd, Wok.	10	B5
Templecombe Ms, Wok.	12	A2
Dorchester Ct		
Ten Acre, Wok.	10	C4
Abercorn Way		
Tenniel Cl, Guil.	18	D6
Testard Rd, Guil.	6	C4
Teviot Cl, Guil.	18	C5
Thistledene, W.Byf.	9	F5
Thorley Cl, W.Byf.	9	G6
Thorley Gdns, Wok.	9	G6
Thorn Bk, Guil.	22	C4
Thornash Cl, Wok.	11	E1
Thornash Rd, Wok.	11	E1
Thornash Way, Wok.	11	E1
Thornton Cl, Guil.	18	C4
Thorpes Cl, Guil.	18	C5
Thorsden Cl, Wok.	11	G4
Thorsden Ct, Wok.	11	G4
Guildford Rd		
Three Gates, Guil.	24	C1
Three Pears Rd, Guil.	24	D2
Thrift Vale, Guil.	20	D5
Thurlton Ct, Wok.	11	G2
Chobham Rd		
Thursby Rd, Wok.	10	C4
Thyme Ct, Guil.	20	B5
Mallow Cres		
Tilehouse Rd, Guil.	23	G6
Tillingbourne Rd, Guil.	27	G6
Tilthams Cor Rd, Gdmg.	26	D5
Tilthams Grn, Gdmg.	26	D5
Timber Cl, Guil.	9	F6
Hacketts La		
Tintagel Way, Wok.	12	A2
Tithebarns La, Wok.	17	G6
Tolldene Cl, Wok.	10	A3
Robin Hood Rd		
Tollgate, Guil.	24	D1
Tolvaddon Cl, Wok.	10	C3
Cardingham		
Tormead Rd, Wok.	23	H2
Torrens Cl, Guil.	18	C5
Torridon Cl, Wok.	10	D3
Tower Cl, Wok.	11	F3
Towing Path, Guil.	23	E6

Name	Pg	Ref
Town Sq, Wok.	11	H3
Church St E		
Townsend La, Wok.	16	B1
St. Peters Rd		
Tracious Cl, Wok.	10	D2
Sythwood		
Tracious La, Wok.	10	D2
Treebys Av, Wok.	19	F2
Tregarth Pl, Wok.	10	B3
Trenance, Wok.	10	C3
Cardingham		
Trentham Cres, Wok.	16	A1
Tresillian Way, Wok.	10	C2
Tresta Wk, Wok.	10	C1
Trevose Av, W.Byf.	9	F6
Triangle, The, Wok.	11	E4
Trigg's Cl, Wok.	11	F5
Trigg's La, Wok.	11	E4
Trinity Chyd, Guil.	7	F3
High St		
Trodd's La, Guil.	25	F3
Trunley Heath Rd, Guil.	27	E6
Tuckey Gro, Wok.	17	F4
Tudor Circle, Gdmg.	26	A6
Tudor Cl, Wok.	12	A3
Tudor Rd, Gdmg.	26	A6
Tunsgate, Guil.	7	F4
Tunsgate Sq Shop Cen, Guil.	7	F4
High St		
Turner Cl, Guil.	19	H5
Turnham Cl, Guil.	23	E6
Turnoak Av, Wok.	11	G6
Turnoak La, Wok.	11	G5
Wych Hill La		
Tychbourne Dr, Guil.	20	C5
Tylehost, Guil.	18	C4
Tynley Gro, Guil.	19	F2
Tyrwhitt Av, Guil.	18	D4
Tythebarn Cl, Guil.	20	B3
Dairyman's Wk		
U		
Unstead La, Guil.	27	E6
Unstead Wd, Guil.	27	E4
Upfolds Grn, Guil.	20	C4
Upper Edgeborough Rd, Guil.	23	H3
Upper Guildown Rd, Guil.	22	D5
Upper Manor Rd, Gdmg.	26	A6
Upperton Rd, Guil.	6	C4
Upshott La, Wok.	13	F3
Upton, Wok.	10	D3
V		
Vale Cl, Wok.	11	G2
The Larches		
Vale Fm Rd, Wok.	11	F3
Valley, The, Guil.	23	E6
Portsmouth Rd		
Venton Cl, Wok.	10	D3
Vernon Way, Guil.	22	B1
Verralls, Wok.	12	B3
Veryan, Wok.	10	C3
Vicarage Gate, Guil.	22	C4
Vicarage La, Wok.	16	C6
Vicarage Rd, Wok.	15	H1
Victoria Rd, Guil.	7	G1
Victoria Rd, Wok.	11	G3
Victoria Way, Wok.	11	G3
Viggory La, Wok.	11	E1
W		
Waggon Cl, Guil.	22	A1
Wakehurst Path, Wok.	8	C6
Waldens Pk Rd, Wok.	11	E2
Waldens Rd, Wok.	11	F3
Walnut Tree Cl, Guil.	6	C1
Walnut Tree Pk, Guil.	23	E2
Waltham Av, Guil.	18	D5
Walton Ct, Wok.	12	A2
Walton Rd, Wok.	11	H2
Walton Ter, Wok.	12	B1
Wansford Grn, Wok.	10	B3
Kenton Way		
Ward St, Guil.	7	F3
Martyr Rd		
Warren La, Wok.	13	H4
Warren Rd, Add.	9	G2
Warren Rd, Gdmg.	26	A6
Warren Rd, Guil.	23	H3
Warrenhyrst, Guil.	24	A3
Warren Rd		
Warwick La, Wok.	10	C5
Warwicks Bench, Guil.	7	F5
Warwicks Bench La, Guil.	7	H6
Warwicks Bench Rd, Guil.	23	G5
Wgter La, Guil.	25	H5
Watercress Way, Wok.	10	D3
Waterden Cl, Guil.	23	H3
Waterden Rd, Guil.	7	H2
Watermead, Wok.	10	B2
Waterside Ms, Guil.	19	E6
Waterside Rd, Guil.	19	F5
Waterside Way, Wok.	10	D4
Winnington Way		
Watersmeet Cl, Guil.	20	A3
Cotts Wd Dr		
Watford Cl, Guil.	23	H2
Waverley Ct, Wok.	11	G4
Wayside Ct, Wok.	10	A2
Langmans Way		
Weald Cl, Guil.	27	G2
Station Rd		
Wealdon Ct, Guil.	22	B2
Humbolt Cl		
Weasdale Ct, Wok.	10	B2
Roundthorn Way		
Websters Cl, Wok.	10	C6
Well Cl, Wok.	11	E3
Well La, Wok.	11	E3
Well Path, Wok.	11	E3
Well La		
Wellington Ter, Wok.	10	A4
Victoria Rd		
Wells Rd, Guil.	20	C5
Wendela Cl, Wok.	11	H4
Wendley Dr, Add.	9	F2
Wendron Cl, Wok.	10	C4
Shilburn Way		
Wendy Cres, Guil.	18	C6
Wentworth Cl, Wok.	17	H1
West Hill Rd, Wok.	11	F5
West Meads, Guil.	22	B3
West Mt, Guil.	6	C5
The Mt		
West Rd, Guil.	7	H2
West St, Wok.	11	H3
Church St E		
Westerfolds Cl, Wok.	12	C2
Westfield Av, Wok.	15	G1
Westfield Common, Wok.	15	G2
Westfield Gro, Wok.	11	H6
Westfield Rd, Guil.	19	G4
Westfield Rd, Wok.	15	F2
Westfield Way, Wok.	15	G2
Westmead, Wok.	10	D3
Weston Cl, Gdmg.	26	A6
Weston Gdns, Wok.	13	E2
Weston Rd, Guil.	22	D1
Weston Way, Wok.	13	E2
Westward Ho, Guil.	19	H6
Westway, Guil.	18	B6
Westwood Av, Add.	9	F4
Westwood Ct, Guil.	22	B1
Hillcrest Rd		
Wexfenne Gdns, Wok.	13	H2
Wey Cl, W.Byf.	9	H5
Broadoaks Cres		
Wey Vw Ct, Guil.	6	C2
Walnut Tree Cl		
Weybrook Dr, Guil.	20	B3
Weydown Cl, Guil.	18	C3
Weydown La, Guil.	18	C3
Cumberland Av		
Weylea Av, Guil.	20	A5
Weyside Gdns, Guil.	18	D6
Weyside Rd, Guil.	18	D6
Weyview Cl, Guil.	19	E6
Wharf La (Send), Wok.	16	C3
Wharf Rd, Guil.	6	D1
Whateley Rd, Guil.	18	D3
Wheatsheaf Cl, Wok.	11	G2
Wherwell Rd, Guil.	6	C4
Whipley Cl, Guil.	20	B3
Weybrook Dr		
White Ho Dr, Guil.	24	B2
White Ho La, Guil.	19	F3
White La, Guil.	24	C4
White Lion Wk Shop Cen, Guil.	7	E3
High St		
White Rose La, Wok.	11	H3
Whitegates, Wok.	11	H6
Loop Rd		
Whitemore Rd, Guil.	19	F4
Whitfield Cl, Guil.	18	C5
Whitmoor Common, Guil.	18	D1
Whitmoor La, Guil.	15	F6
Whopshott Av, Wok.	11	E2
Whopshott Cl, Wok.	11	E2
Whopshott Dr, Wok.	11	E2
Wilbury Rd, Wok.	11	F3
Wildbank Cl, Wok.	11	H4
White Rose La		
Wilderness Rd, Guil.	22	B3
Wilders Cl, Wok.	11	E4
Wildwood Cl, Wok.	13	F1
Wilfred St, Wok.	11	F4
William Rd, Guil.	6	D1
William Russell Ct, Wok.	10	A4
Raglan Rd		
William Swayne Pl, Guil.	7	G2
Station App		
Williams Wk, Guil.	18	D4
Grange Rd		
Willow Bk, Wok.	15	G2
Willow Cl, Add.	9	F3
Willow Dr, Wok.	17	G4
Willow La, Guil.	24	A1
Boxgrove Rd		
Willow Rd, Gdmg.	26	B5
Willow Way, Guil.	18	D4
Willow Way, Wok.	15	F1
Willowmead Cl, Wok.	10	C2
Willows, The, Guil.	20	D6
Collier Way		
Wilson Way, Wok.	11	F2
Windgates, Guil.	20	C5
Tychbourne Dr		
Winds Ridge, Wok.	16	C5
Windsor Cl, Guil.	22	B4
Windsor Way, Guil.	12	C2
Wingfield Cl, Add.	9	H2
Winnards, Wok.	10	D4
Abercorn Way		
Winnington Way, Wok.	10	D4
Winston Way, Wok.	12	B6
Winterhill Way, Guil.	20	B4
Wishbone Way, Wok.	10	B2
Withies, The, Wok.	10	A3
Wodeland Av, Guil.	6	A5
Woking Business Pk, Wok.	12	B1
Woking Rd, Guil.	19	F3
Wolsey Pl Shop Cen, Wok.	11	G3
Commercial Way		
Wolsey Wk, Wok.	11	G3
Wonersh Common, Guil.	28	B3
Wonersh Common Rd, Guil.	28	B4
Wood Riding, Wok.	13	F1
Pyrford Wds Rd		
Wood Ri, Guil.	18	A6
Wood Rd, Gdmg.	26	B6
Woodbridge Hill, Guil.	22	D1
Woodbridge Hill Gdns, Guil.	22	C1
Woodbridge Meadows, Guil.	23	E1
Woodbridge Rd, Guil.	23	E1
Woodcote, Guil.	22	D6
Woodend Cl, Wok.	10	C5
Woodger Cl, Guil.	20	C6
Kingfisher Dr		
Woodham La, Add.	9	A6
Woodham La, Wok.	8	B6
Woodham Pk Rd, Add.	9	F1
Woodham Pk Way, Add.	9	F3
Woodham Rd, Wok.	11	G1
Woodham Waye, Wok.	8	B5
Woodhill, Wok.	17	H5
Woodland Vw, Gdmg.	26	A4
Woodlands, Wok.	11	G4
Constitution Hill		
Woodlands Av, W.Byf.	9	F5
Woodlands Cl, Cher.	8	B2
Woodlands Ct, Wok.	11	G5
Constitution Hill		
Woodlands Pk, Guil.	20	B6
Woodlands Pk, Wok.	8	C6
Blackmore Cres		
Woodlands Rd, Guil.	19	F4
Woodlands Rd, W.Byf.	9	F6
Woodlawn Gro, Wok.	11	H1
Woodmancote Gdns, W.Byf.	9	G5
Woodpecker Way, Wok.	15	F3
Woodruff Av, Guil.	20	A5
Woodside Rd, Guil.	22	B1
Woodstock, Guil.	21	H2
Woodstock, Wok.	11	G2
Woodway, Guil.	24	B1
Woodyers Cl, Guil.	28	B6
Worcester Rd, Guil.	18	B6
Worplesdon Rd, Guil.	18	B3
Worsfold Cl, Wok.	16	B3
Wych Elm Ri, Guil.	7	G6
Wych Hill, Wok.	11	E5
Wych Hill La, Wok.	11	G5
Wych Hill Pk, Wok.	11	F5
Wych Hill Ri, Wok.	11	E5
Wych Hill Way, Wok.	11	F6
Wykeham Rd, Guil.	24	D1
Wyndham Rd, Wok.	10	D4
Y		
Yarrowfield, Wok.	15	F3
Yew Tree Dr, Guil.	19	E4
York Rd, Guil.	7	E2
York Rd, Wok.	11	G4